D0615566

Finding Your Inner Mama

Finding Your Inner Mama

~

WOMEN REFLECT ON THE CHALLENGES AND REWARDS OF MOTHERHOOD

Edited by
EDEN STEINBERG

Trumpeter
BOSTON & LONDON 2007

Trumpeter Books
An imprint of
Shambhala Publications, Inc.
Horticultural Hall
300 Massachusetts Avenue
Boston, Massachusetts 02115
www.shambhala.com

This book was previously published in hardcover
under the title *Your Children Will Raise You.*

Pages 253–256 constitute an extension of the copyright page.

9 8 7 6 5 4 3 2 1

First Paperback Edition

Printed in the United States of America

⊗This edition is printed on acid-free paper that meets the American
National Standards Institute Z39.48 Standard.

Distributed in the United States by Random House, Inc., and in
Canada by Random House of Canada Ltd

Library of Congress Cataloging-in-Publication Data
Finding your inner mama; women reflect on the challenges and rewards of
motherhood/edited by Eden Steinberg.—1st pbk. ed.
p. cm.
Rev. ed. of: Your children will raise you. Boston: Trumpeter, 2005.
Includes bibliographical references.
ISBN 978-1-59030-423-5
1. Motherhood. 2. Mothers—psychology. 3. Mother and child.
4. Motherhood—religious aspects. I. Steinberg, Eden.
II. Your children will raise you.
HQ759.F473 2007
306.874′3—dc22
2006053257

For my mother, Grace—your strength and intellectual curiosity have been an inspiration to me; thank you for all your love and support

And for Nina, Liza, Kate, and Genya—the new generation of mothers in our family who are all finding their way with grace and courage; it's wonderful to be in this together

"Motherhood is not what we imagined. It is more delightful, more heartbreaking. . . . It is not the calm after the storm we have been led to expect. It is almost more than a person can bear. *Almost.*"

—Ariel Gore, *The Mother Trip*

CONTENTS

ACKNOWLEDGMENTS   ix

INTRODUCTION   xi

Part One
THE REALITY OF BEING A MOTHER

Writings from a Birth Year *Louise Erdrich*	3
A Crash Course in Vulnerability and	
Other Lessons *Harriet Lerner*	13
Anger and Tenderness *Adrienne Rich*	26
Giving Birth to Ambivalence *Andrea J. Buchanan*	32
My Daughter at Fourteen *Carolyn Magner Mason*	39
The Way I Dreamed It *Ariel Gore*	43
One Week until College *Sandi Kahn Shelton*	50

Part Two
THE INNER WORK OF MOTHERHOOD

Dawn *Rabbi Nancy Fuchs-Kreimer*	59
Children as Spiritual Teachers *Cheryl Dimof*	68
Responding to "Bad" Behavior *Wendy Mogel*	76
Parenting with Mindful Awareness *Myla and Jon Kabat-Zinn*	90
Recognizing Our Hidden Wounds *Harville Hendrix and*	
Helen LaKelly Hunt	99

CONTENTS

The Sacred Chaos of Parenthood   *Carolyn R. Gimian*   114

"Exceptional" Mothering in a "Normal" World

　Miriam Greenspan   126

Part Three
WHY IS BEING A MOTHER SO HARD?

Guilt—What It Does to Us   *Anne Roiphe*   147

The New Momism   *Susan J. Douglas and*

　Meredith W. Michaels   157

Power Moms and the Problem of Overparenting

　Joan K. Peters   176

Claiming the Joy   *Daphne de Marneffe*   189

Part Four
FINDING BALANCE

Tell Your Secrets   *Ariel Gore*   203

Simplicity   *Katrina Kenison*   207

I'm Breathing, Are You?   *Nancy Hathaway*   214

Good-bye Herd   *Muffy Mead-Ferro*   225

Time-Out for Parents   *Cheri Huber and Melinda Guyol*   235

Sitting in Happy   *Denise Roy*   244

CONTRIBUTORS   247

CREDITS   253

ACKNOWLEDGMENTS

Many thanks to my colleagues at Shambhala for their support and enthusiasm. Special thanks to Ben Gleason and Katie Keach, for their able assistance, and to my editors Beth Frankl and Peter Turner, for their insightful feedback.

I'd also like to thank:

Rich Borofsky, for introducing me to the idea of parenthood as spiritual practice

Caroline, for making it possible for me to leave home

Nathan and Oliver, my two sons, for helping me to grow up

And Peter, my husband, for his extraordinary love, support, and sense of humor.

INTRODUCTION

IT'S BEEN SAID THAT WE WRITE THE BOOKS we need to read. In this case, I've edited the book I desperately need to read. This collection of writings was born out of a burning desire to reflect on the rich and challenging experience of motherhood. When I became a mother, I realized that my life had taken a new and powerful direction. Motherhood was not what I had expected: I didn't get the smiling, chubby baby in the Gerber commercial (who, I now realize, was probably close to a year old). I got a newborn. A tiny, thin baby who seemed unimaginably vulnerable, who slept only an hour-and-a-half at a time, who sometimes cried inconsolably, who grew and changed and developed so quickly I could barely keep up. I quickly found myself face-to-face with my deepest hopes and fears, and uncomfortably aware of my limitations.

Four years later, I don't have the polite, compliant, appreciative preschooler I had planned for, either. My image of family life did not include my four-year-old son grabbing his one-year-old brother by the neck, and, upon being told to stop it immediately, him running away from me yelling, "I don't like you, Mommy!" This far into the journey of motherhood, I am truly humbled, knee-deep in shattered dreams—and I am also growing up in important ways.

Soon after my first son was born, I began to look for books that spoke to the intensity of the experience I was having as a new mother. There are, of course, innumerable books on parenting, but the majority of these are about child development and the do's and don'ts of effective parenting. I quickly found that only a handful of books spoke of the tumultuous inner experience of motherhood itself.

Early motherhood can be a real crisis. In addition to the significant physical challenges of caring for a new baby, there are the waves of powerful emotion, a profound identity shift, a sort of existential crisis: Who am I now? What does it mean to be a mother? How am I going to do this? Like my mother did it? *Not* like my mother did it? What or who can guide me through all the joy, pain, change, and uncertainty? Most books I found in the parenting section didn't satisfy my need to explore these kinds of questions.

As I started to look around for guidance, I saw mostly romanticized representations of motherhood. In books, magazines, and television we see the perfect mom: calm, confident, unconditionally wise, unconditionally loving, part early childhood educator, part child psychologist, part Martha Stewart. I couldn't relate to this image at all, and yet many of the young mothers I was meeting had a tendency to reinforce and project this perfect-mom ideal. For this reason, I was so very grateful to the women who were able to be candid about the realities of motherhood, including the darker side that had so surprised me: the frustrations, the insecurities, the disappointments. Talking to these women, I felt much less defective and alone.

And, little by little, I began to discover other helpful resources. I found books, articles, and essays that spoke to the lived experience of motherhood in realistic and profound terms. I also had the good fortune of knowing two wise, older parents, both longtime practitioners of Zen Buddhism, who introduced me to the idea that parenthood could be undertaken as a form of spiritual practice, of meditation practice. This became a compelling idea for me, one that I wanted to explore further, and so I began to look for writings that explored motherhood in spiritual and transformative terms.

The book you're holding is the result of my search. It offers a variety of writings that capture the rich, inner experience of motherhood—writings that see beyond the gauzy, romantic ideals to glimpse motherhood as different and much more than we thought: as a profound opportunity for self-understanding, personal growth, and real wisdom.

The collection is divided into four parts. In part 1, "The Reality of Being a Mother," women get beyond the myths and ideals to look honestly at the mixture of joy, heartache, confusion, love, anger, fear, and passion that is motherhood. These selections describe the lived experience of motherhood during its most intensive years, from giving birth to the empty nest. I've included a short excerpt from Adrienne Rich's groundbreaking memoir of motherhood, *Of Woman Born*, first published in 1976, in which she spoke boldly and openly of motherhood's dark side, of the unsettling mixture of resentment and love that she felt for her three children. It is remarkable that almost thirty years later we seem to be struggling to overcome the same stereotypes and taboos that Rich sought to question and dismantle.

Part 2 is titled "The Inner Work of Motherhood." The contributors to this section speak from a variety of religious traditions on the topic of how we can understand and experience motherhood as a spiritually transformative journey. But why bring religion into it? Looking deeply at our experience as mothers, we are continually called upon to grow and develop as people—to become more compassionate, more aware, more flexible, more accepting of ourselves and others. In short, motherhood demands that we become better people. Some women are discovering profound connections between the lessons of motherhood and the truths articulated by their religious traditions. These women have come to view motherhood as a form of spiritual training, as cleverly conveyed in the book title *My Monastery Is a Minivan* (written by Denise Roy, a graduate of a Jesuit seminary and a mother of four). The writings in this section of the book are about discovering wisdom and insight in the midst of the ordinary, daily routines of mothering.

Readers will note that there are a number of selections by Buddhist authors in this section (and sprinkled throughout this collection). At first glance, you might not expect Buddhism, a tradition that has historically been monastic in emphasis—and whose founder abandoned his own wife and child to pursue enlightenment—to have much to say about motherhood. The Buddha named his own child Rahula, which means "fetter," though, to be fair, he had not yet reached enlightenment at the time. Yet Buddhist teaching has long emphasized the view that ordinary, daily life can be rich ground for spiritual awakening. The Buddhist writings presented here will be meaningful and relevant to women of any religious tradition.

Part 3 is titled "Why Is Being a Mother So Hard?" These writings explore the vexing problems of guilt, unrealistic images of motherhood in the media, the trend of over-parenting, as well as restrictive stereotypes and our tendency to reinforce them. Daphne de Marneffe, author of the compelling book *Maternal Desire*, explores a more hidden problem: the difficulty we may have in fully experiencing the rich pleasures of motherhood. Mothering includes tremendous challenges and awesome beauty. De Marneffe reminds us that our work as mothers is to open up to all of it. The writings in this section of the book are somewhat academic and sociological, but they are well worth the reader's effort. They provide a broader perspective and much food for thought about our experience as mothers.

Part 4, "Finding Balance," offers some specific techniques and approaches to finding sanity and solid ground as a mother. I'm wary of any parenting dos and don'ts—the way we parent is so personal, so unique to each mother and child—but this section of the book does offer some advice and guidance from spiritual teachers and everyday moms on finding center in a job that often throws us off balance.

A few weeks after I gave birth to my first child, in the thick of my exhaustion, worrying whether I was doing everything right, whether or not my baby would live through the night, I realized something. I realized that if I was going to survive this thing, I was going to have to grow and change. First of all, I was going to have to let go of a lot of things I felt entitled to: uninterrupted sleep; things going as planned; a feeling of being in command, the master of my circumstances. I also saw that I was ultimately going to have to let go of my very self-concept, my idea of motherhood, and my expectations of my child. All of it had to go.

The idea of shedding all of these burdens was exciting. The thought itself was a relief. And it suddenly dawned on me that my whole concept of motherhood had been wrong. I thought that as a mother I would carefully mold and shape my children. If I did my job right, my children would turn out to be well-adjusted, loving, thoughtful, and interesting people. As it turns out, motherhood is molding and shaping *me*. At the end of all this, I am the one who could end up well-adjusted, loving, thoughtful, and interesting.

In different ways, the writings in this collection explain how this might be true, how our experiences as mothers can lead us to valuable insight and transformation. So with this collection I respectfully suggest to all of you that, from a certain perspective, your children will raise you. That's good news, isn't it?

EDEN STEINBERG
Boston, Massachusetts

Part One

~

The Reality of Being a Mother

Writings from a Birth Year

Louise Erdrich

For most women, the experience of giving birth is beyond description. How could we fully convey the mystery, the longing, the joy? Only a writer of Louise Erdrich's talent can pull it off. At last someone has amply captured the wonder and awe of early motherhood, as only a skilled poet and novelist could.

~

WE CONCEIVE OUR CHILDREN in deepest night, in blazing sun, outdoors, in barns and alleys and minivans. We have no rules, no ceremonies, we don't even need a driver's license. Conception is often something of a by-product of sex, a candle in a one-room studio, pure brute chance, a wonder. To make love with the desire for a child is to move the act out of its singularity, to make the need of the moment an eternal wish. But of all passing notions, that of a human being for a child is perhaps the purest in the abstract, and the most complicated in reality. Growing, bearing, mothering or fathering, supporting, and at last letting go of an infant is a powerful and mundane creative act that rapturously sucks up whole chunks of life.

Other parents—among them, the first female judge appointed in New Hampshire, my own midwife, a perpetually overwhelmed movie researcher and television producer, and our neighbor, who baby-sits to make a difficult living—seem surprised at their own helplessness in the face of the passion they feel for their children. We live and work with a divided consciousness. It is a beautiful enough shock to fall in love with another adult, to feel the possibility of unbearable sorrow at the loss of that other, essential, personality, expressed just so, that particular touch. But love of an infant is of a different order. It is twinned love, all absorbing, a blur of boundaries and messages. It is uncomfortably close to self-erasure, and in the face of it one's fat ambitions, desperations, private icons, and urges fall away into a dreamlike *before* that haunts and forces itself into the present with tough persistence.

The self will not be forced under, nor will the baby's needs gracefully retreat. The world tips away when we look into our children's faces. The days flood by. Time with children runs through our fingers like water as we lift our hands, try to hold, to capture, to fix moments in a lens, a magic circle of images or words. We snap photos, videotape, memorialize while we experience a fast-forward in which there is no replay of even a single instant.

We have a baby. Our sixth child, our third birth. During that year, our older, adopted children hit adolescence like runaway trucks. Dear grandparents weaken and die. Michael rises at four in the morning, hardly seems to sleep at all. To keep the door to the other self—the writing self—open, I scratch messages on the envelopes of letters I can't answer, in the margins of books I'm too tired to review. On pharmacy prescription bags, dime-store notebooks, children's construction paper, I keep writing.

One reason there is not a great deal written about what it is like to be the mother of a new infant is that there is rarely a moment to think of anything else besides that infant's needs. Endless time with a small baby is spent asking, *What do you want? What do you want?* The sounds of her unhappiness range from mild yodeling to extended bawls. *What do you want?* Our baby's cries are not monotonous. They seem quite purposeful, though hard to describe. They are a language that changes every week, one so primal that the meaning I gather is purely physical. I do what she "tells" me to do—feed, burp, change, amuse, distract, hold, help, look at, help to sleep, reassure—without consciously choosing to do it. I take her instructions without translating her meaning into words, but simply bypass straight to action. My brain is a white blur. I lose track of what I've been doing, where I've been, who I am.

CRYING

Walking. Walking. Walking. Rocking her while her cries fill me. They rise like water. A part of me has been formed and released and set upon the earth to wail. Her cries are painful to me, physically hard to take. Her cries hurt my temples, my breasts. I often cry along if I cannot comfort her. What else is there to do? This morning she falls asleep, finally, as I rock her. Sucking her favorite three fingers, she drifts. All of the tension leaves her small, round, tender body. She goes heavy against me. In this old chair, woven of tough bent willow, I keep rocking her. My chance to work has come, but I hate to put her down.

I'm an instinctive mother, not a book-read one, and my feeling is that a baby must be weaned slowly from its other body—mine. So

I keep her close, sleep with her curled tight, tie her onto me with padded contraptions. My days here have become sensuous, suffused with the particular, which is not to say that they aren't difficult, or that I get much done. With each birth I have been thrown into a joy of the physical emotions, a religious and fixated delight that seizes me so thoroughly the life of the imagination sometimes seems a spare place. The grounded pleasures—nursing, touching the exquisite fontanel of our baby, a yellow-pink fragrance of sun-heated cotton and tepid cream, gazing eternally into her mystery eyes—are only tempered by sleep deprivation. We know why prisoners break more easily without sleep. *I give up, I'll tell you anything,* I want to say to her sometimes, nearly weeping.

NESTS

I have one nest of Eastern phoebe construction—mud and emerald moss, a failed attempt that fell off a too slick wall, a comfortable looking silver nest constructed of the down of milkweed pods, a loose swirl of long hairs plucked from the tails of our neighbor's brown and white horses. I have the nest of a Baltimore oriole, a long gray sack with a bottleneck, woven to a budded apple branch, a very special nest that my father at sixty-eight risked his neck climbing a high tree to collect for me. I have a tight little nest including plastic tinsel and my mother's pink-blue knitting yarn, a heavy robin's nest of thick muck and flower stems, and a cup of grass and shredded Kleenex. I suppose I could include my wasp nests, the silt cones, the paper bowls, the great gray combed rose I cut from a year-old sumac. I collect nests in late fall when the leaves are off the trees. On my shelves, there are quite a few nests, collected casually year by year. I prize above them all the nest constructed of my daughters' hair.

My mother gave me the idea two springs ago. I saw her draping yarn on the flowering crab apple tree just outside the kitchen window, and the following fall I found the nest containing those very leftovers from a scarf she had been knitting. All last winter, just before breakfast each morning, I brushed the dark brown, the golden, the medium brown hair of our daughters smooth, and all winter I saved the cleanings from the brush in a small paper bag that I emptied by the stump in the yard last spring.

It was not until the leaves fell off and the small trees bent nakedly beside the road that I saw it, a small cup in a low shrub, held in the fork of a twisting branch.

Now, as I am setting the nest on a shelf in the light of an eastern window, our middle daughter's blond hair gleams, then the roan highlights in the rich brown of the eldest's and perhaps a bit of our baby's fine grass-pale floss. It is a tight woven nest that kept its shape through the autumn rain. It is a deep cup, an indigo bunting's water tight nest, perhaps, or a finch's.

It is almost too painful to hold the nest, too rich, as life often is with children. I see the bird, quick breathing, small, thrilling like a heart. I hear its song, high and clear, beating in its throat. I see that bird alone in the nest woven from the hair of my daughters, and I cannot hold the nest because longing seizes me. Not only do I feel how quickly they are growing from the curved shape of my arms when holding them, but I want to sit in the presence of my own mother so badly I feel my heart will crack.

Life seems to flood by, taking our loves quickly in its flow. In the growth of children, in the aging of beloved parents, time's chart is magnified, shown in its particularity, focused, so that with each celebration of maturity there is also a pang of loss. This is our human problem, one common to parents, sons and daughters, too—how to let go while holding tight, how to simultaneously cherish the closeness and intricacy of the bond while at the same time letting out the raveling string, the red yarn that ties our hearts.

Sleepwalkers

Perhaps I've passed on my edgy sleeping habits to our baby. She is a light sleeper and our presences wake her continually. She has outgrown the bassinet next to our bed—she bumps its sides rolling over, waking herself to fret. And so, for the first night since she was conceived, she sleeps more than a foot away.

First she was part of me, and then she slept curled between us. Then, a night, I don't know when, she was placed in her bassinet. Now she sleeps in the next room. For nights I wake, startled, my brain humming with abysmal exhaustion, aware only in the most atavistic way that something is wrong. It is as if in sleep I have been cut in two and suddenly I miss my other half. I am there at her cry and in the deepest hour of the night we fit together again like the pieces of a broken locket. On a cot in her little room, warming gradually under webs of afghans, we nurse, sighing, becoming more separate with every breath.

The air is moving and the leaves are talking. Somewhere in the darkness of the stripped bed of the new pond a shrill killdeer's piping. Rumble of a car passing once, twice, silence. I am sleeping hard, rolled at an angle against my husband. In the hour of the wolf our door opens and it is our five-year-old whispering in fear—another awful dream. She creeps close and I hoist her against me. Warm, she clings tight and soon her sharp breathing falls away. The night goes on. I do not sleep because it is unbearably good to lie there, witnessing in peace the oblivion of those I love. She's calmer now, lighting into sleep soft as a moth. He is dark and solid shale reaching down through the foundation and the beams of the ground. Tonight, I am more darkness through which their two bodies have passed and fused.

ALL MOTHERS

I see myself frozen in a clutch of mothers, in a flock, a panic of mothers, in a spongy-shoed group who manage all of the trivia of motherhood—the skills and lessons that must be learned, the clothes stitched and bruises kissed—with seemingly greater ease than I ever achieve. The truth is, I like doing these small things, up to a point, but when the sludge of incremental necessities becomes suffocating, I rebel and let the details slide. How glad I am to know that I am not the only one. From outside, the mothers in brilliant parkas look affable and competent, but as I sit talking among them I come to know that we are all struggling, with more or less grace, to hold on to the tiger tail of children's, husband's, parents', and siblings' lives while at the same time saving a little core of self in our own, just enough to live by.

In talking to other women over years, I begin to absorb them somehow, as if we're all permeable. Some days I'm made up of a thousand mothers who have given one ironic look, one laugh at the right moment, one exasperated wave, one acknowledgment. Mothering is a subtle art whose rhythm we collect and learn, as much from one another as by instinct. Taking shape, we shape each other, with subtle pressures and sudden knocks. The challenges shape us, approvals refine, the wear and tear of small abrasions transform until we're slowly made up of one another and yet wholly ourselves.

Our baby is almost a year old, and down to one or two breast-feedings a day. If we miss one, she begins to suck my collar cuffs, makes cloth nipples between her fists and wet marks on my shirt. I soothe myself with her need, too, for I hate to wean her. Time stops around us for a moment, scenes held in a snowy globe. Hold back! Stop! I panic, unprepared for change, but it's too late. She sweeps on in her life. I cannot gather back one moment, only marvel at what comes next.

I am keeping track for baby, waiting for her to dream something that she can put into words. There are spaces on the baby calendar for the first tooth, the first smile, the first word, but nowhere to record the first dream. I leave space in the margins and wait. She has been dreaming all along, there is no question watching her face complex in sleep, her eyes moving under delicate, violet-pink, sunrise lids.

Grand elk moving underneath the grand sky. Tyrant blue jays. Cats loping bannerlike across the fields. Moths fanning their pale wings against the light. Spiders. Brown recluse, marked like a violin. The beating of a heart perhaps, moving in, moving out. My own voice—perhaps she dreams my own voice as I dream hers—starting out of sleep, awake, certain that she's cried out.

For years now I have been dreaming the powerful anxiety dreams of all parents. Something is lost, something must be protected. A baby swims in an aquarium, a baby sleeps in a suitcase. The suitcase goes astray, the airline company will not return it. I spend all night arguing with people at a baggage claims desk. Parents endure exhausing nights searching drawers and running through corridors and town streets and emptying laundry baskets looking for their missing babies. Mine is hiding in a washing machine or behind a Corinthian column or out in the long grass, the endless grass. Mine is running toward the nameless sky.

WALKING

To pull herself upright, to strain upward, to climb, has been baby's obsession for the past three months and now, on her first birthday, it is that urge I celebrate and fear. She has pulled herself erect by the strings of her sister's hair, by using my clothes, hands, earrings, by the edges and the rungs and the unstable handles of the world. She has yanked herself up, stepped, and it is clear from her grand excitement that walking is one of the most important things we ever do. It is raw power to go forward, to lunge, catching at important arms and hands, to take control of the body, tell it what to do, to leave behind the immobility of babyhood. With each step she swells, her breath goes ragged and her eyes darken in a shine of happiness. A glaze of physical joy covers her, moves through her, more intense than the banged forehead, bumped chin, the bruises and knocks and losses, even than the breathtaking falls and solid thumps, joy more powerful than good sense.

It would seem she has everything she could want—she is fed, she is carried, she is rocked, put to sleep. But no, *walking* is the thing, the consuming urge to seize control. She has to walk to gain entrance to the world. From now on, she will get from here to there more and more by her own effort. As she goes, she will notice worn grass, shops or snow or the shape of trees. She will walk for reasons other than to get somewhere in particular. She'll walk to think or not to think, to leave the body, which is often the same as becoming at one with it. She will walk to ward off anger in its many forms. For pleasure, purpose, or to grieve. She'll walk until the world slows down, until her brain lets go of everything behind and until her eyes see only the next step. She'll walk until her feet hurt, her muscles tremble, until her eyes are numb with looking. She'll walk until her sense of balance is the one thing left and the rest of the world is balanced, too, and eventually, if we do the growing up right, she will walk away from us.

A Crash Course in Vulnerability and Other Lessons

Harriet Lerner

Lerner is a psychologist and the author of numerous insightful books about families' and women's emotional lives. Her writing on mother-hood has a wonderful sense of honesty, perspective, and humor. Here she explains how raising children can teach us some of life's most valuable lessons.

~

*I*BECAME PREGNANT IN THE old-fashioned way. I never be-lieved that I would *really* become pregnant because the thought of having an entire person grow inside your body is such a bizarre idea that only lunatics or religious fanatics would take for granted the fact that it might actually happen. And then there is the matter of getting the baby out, which is something no normal person wants to think about.

I was thirty when I became pregnant for the first time. Before this pregnancy, I had not experienced one maternal twinge. When my friends would bring their infants in little carrying baskets to dinner parties, I felt sorry for them (the parents) because the whole thing seemed like so much trouble. "Oh, yes," I would chirp with false enthusiasm when asked if I would like to hold one of these tiny babies. But I was just being polite or trying to do the normal-appearing thing. I always sat down before allowing anyone to hand me a baby because I'm something of a klutz and I knew that if anyone was going to drop a baby it would be me.

To say that I was not maternal is an understatement of vast proportion. I enjoyed adult company, and my idea of a good time did not include hanging out with babies who were unable to dress themselves, use the toilet, or make interesting conversation. By contrast, my husband, Steve, truly loved babies and never worried about dropping them. We always planned to have children, but not, on my part, out of any heartfelt desire. I just thought that having children was an important life experience I shouldn't miss out on, anymore than I wanted to miss out on live concerts or traveling through Europe. Although I thought having children seemed like the thing to do, I put it off as long as I reasonably could.

As soon as I got the news that I was pregnant, however, I was bursting with self-importance and pride. I wanted to grab strangers in the supermarket and say, "Hey, I may look like a regular person, but I'm *pregnant,* you know!" The fact that other women had done this before me didn't make it feel any less like a miraculous personal achievement.

My confidence inflated even more when I sailed through my first trimester without a flicker of nausea or discomfort. I took credit for the fact that things were moving along so swimmingly, and I concluded that this was a "good sign," that maybe I was suited to motherhood after all.

But at the beginning of my second trimester I began spotting, then bleeding. My doctor asked if I wanted to consider having an abortion because the baby's risk of brain damage was significant. Sometimes I wouldn't bleed at all and I'd be filled with hope, and sometimes I'd *really* bleed and think that I—or the baby—was dying. I felt panic-stricken, filled with a mixture of terror for our dual survival and of utter humiliation at the prospect of ruining someone's expensive couch.

I consulted with an expert at the University of Kansas Medical Center, then transferred to the best obstetrician in Topeka, one with outstanding diagnostic skills who did not think my baby would be brain damaged. Basically the whole thing was a gamble. We didn't know whether enough of the placenta would stay attached, because it had become implanted too low and was shearing off as the pregnancy progressed. There is probably a more medically accurate way to describe what was happening, but this is how I understood my situation at the time. I had a healthy fetus in utero, and I thought that the medical profession, as advanced as it was, should know how to make a placenta stay put. It seemed like a minor technicality that needn't have life-or-death consequences.

Containing my anxiety was not easy. When I was five months' pregnant, Steve and I were watching a late-night adventure story about a group of people trapped in the elevator of a high-rise building. The bad guy, lurking above them in the elevator shaft, was severing the steel cables that held the cabin. Panic spread among the occupants as they swung about, their lives now hanging by a thread. What a stupid, boring plot, I thought. Seconds later, I felt as if I couldn't breathe. I told Steve I was about to faint or I was having a heart attack or I was simply going to die. "Call the doctor at home!" I commanded my frightened husband. "Wake him up!"

"It sounds like you're hyperventilating, doesn't it?" the doctor said when I had composed myself enough to describe my symptoms. I should have put my head in a paper bag. Now that it was determined that I would live, I was embarrassed that we had awakened him at midnight—two psychologists failing to recognize the ordinary symptoms of anxiety. The television show must have triggered my terror about what was happening within my own body. The image of people trapped in an elevator with the weakened cords threatening to plunge them to their death stayed with me for a long time.

Having a baby was now almost all I cared about. I wanted this baby with a fierceness I had not known was possible, and I would burst into tears if I found myself in line at the supermarket with a mother and her infant. I'm not sentimental about fetuses, so there was no way I could have anticipated the searing intensity of this bond and the devastation I felt at the prospect of my loss. I desperately, desperately, desperately wanted this baby, but what I got was a crash course in feeling totally vulnerable and helpless. Indeed, having children, even in so-called ordinary circumstances, is a lifelong lesson in feeling out of control. So if you're one of those total control freaks, I advise you at all costs to avoid making or adopting a baby.

I was told to expect a cesarean section and a premature birth, but as an act of hope, Steve and I took a natural childbirth class at a local hospital. Apart from us, it consisted of normal couples having normal pregnancies. The teacher appeared to be the sort of person who would never herself do anything as messy as giving birth, and she spoke with that false brightness some people reserve for addressing the very old and the very young. The word *woman* was not in her vocabulary. It was always *lady*, as in "A *lady* may notice a bloodstained mucous discharge at the start of labor," or, in the plural, "You *ladies* will have your pubic hair shaved when you are admitted to the hospital."

During every class, I considered approaching her politely to suggest that she try out the word *woman*—maybe just once or twice—but I never gathered the requisite courage. I still had sporadic bleeding, my nerves were shot, and I had become wildly superstitious, so I was convinced that the entire placenta would shear right off my uterine wall if I upset this teacher with my radical feminist demands.

I did raise my hand in class to ask a couple of questions, actually the same question in two ways: "How do you *know* when you are going into labor?" and "What do contractions *feel* like when they first begin?" To each inquiry, the teacher responded, "Some ladies say it feels like *menstrual cramps*." I paid careful attention to her answer, because I tend to be absentminded. I certainly didn't want suddenly to find the baby's head sticking out when I wasn't paying attention because by then it would be too late for my cesarean section, which I had been told might be necessary to save my baby's life and my own. Absentmindedness aside, though, I felt terrified in the face of my inability to ensure that the baby—or I—would be okay.

Surrender

Only much later would I come to understand that I needed to surrender to the fear—that pregnancy and childbirth inevitably teach us about surrending to forces greater than ourselves. Surrender is not the American way, and most people have negative associations to the very word. To surrender is to lose, to throw our hands up in the air to admit defeat. Instead, our cultural orientation requires us to be in control. Men are supposed to be in charge of other men, women, and nature. Women are supposed to control their children, as if we could. Surrender has connotations of giving up, failing, rather than of giving ourselves over to forces or events larger than we are.

It's the American way to believe that every problem has a solution and that every obstacle can be overcome. We believe that we're in charge of our own destiny, that we get what we deserve. When things get rough, we can try harder, make a new plan, think positively, and bootstrap our way to success. Everything that goes wrong can be fixed, if not by us, then surely by the doctor (or therapist, rabbi, priest, or healer). Much of the pain and grief that mothers feel stems from the belief that we should have control over our children, when it is hard enough to have control over ourselves.

Up until the time my pregnancy became prefixed by the word *complicated*, I assumed that my adult life would go as I planned, that nothing really bad would ever happen to me. Intellectually, I knew this wasn't so, because bad things happen to everyone, and indeed, some bad things had already happened to me. But I secretly believed that I could surely get pregnancy right, if I only put my mind to it. In reality, pregnancy is an event largely beyond our control, and there is no one right or wrong way to move through the experience.

How *can* we best prepare for pregnancy? Consider the voice of one new mother:

> As soon as I learned I was pregnant, I read everything I could get my hands on. I wanted to be as fully informed

as possible. I became an expert on fetal development. I studied the biological, hormonal, and emotional aspects of pregnancy. I read everything about childbirth. I wanted to know exactly what was happening to my body and what I could expect each step of the way. When I wasn't reading, I was talking to other women and getting advice. For me, knowledge was power.

In contrast, a mother of two shared the following words with me:

As soon as I let people know I was pregnant, other women began to tell me their personal stories. I didn't ask them to share their experiences, and I didn't particularly want to listen. I wanted to trust the universe, to see my pregnancy as a normal process that did not require me to become some kind of expert. I read nothing on the subject, because I just wanted to be in the moment. I didn't want to get trapped by false expectations or future fears. If I heard the horror stories, they would only scare me. If I heard about perfect pregnancies, I'd feel angry if mine didn't go that way. I had the basic information from my doctor on prenatal care. I prepared for natural childbirth. I knew the essentials. Beyond that, I just wanted to experience whatever happened.

These two women may sound as different as night and day, but their stories simply reflect opposite sides of the same coin. Both are describing their coping style in the face of a catastrophic experience. By *catastrophe*, I don't mean disaster or tragedy. In this context, catastrophe refers to "the poignant enormity of our life experience," as Jon Kabat-Zinn explains in his book *Full Catastrophe Living.*

Pregnancy and childbirth can be either heartbreaking or exhilarating. The same is true of the process of adoption. Whether these journeys go smoothly or not, there is no other normative experience in our lives, apart from our own birth and death, that puts us through such massive change and transformation in such a relatively brief amount of time. The challenge is to embrace the full experience, and sometimes just to get through it as best we can.

When things go by the book, which statistically speaking they are likely to do, pregnancy is still a lesson in surrender and vulnerability. Your body is inhabited; you live with the realization that childbirth is a wild card; and you know at some level that your life will soon be altered in ways you cannot even begin to imagine. No matter how well you prepare yourself, you are not going to be able to run the show. You're in the thick of a full catastrophe, and change is the only thing you can count on for sure.

AND ALL OF THIS LEADS TO . . . A BABY!?

With so much anxiety about the pregnancy itself, I had almost forgotten that the end result might be a baby. But on June 5, 1975, I woke up in the middle of the night and noted to my amazement that I was having menstrual cramps. I racked my brain to figure out how for godsake I could possibly be having menstrual cramps when I couldn't even remember having my last period. But I figured everything was going wrong anyway, so here was just one more bit of weirdness from my entirely untrustworthy body. I considered searching for the Midol but then remembered that pregnant ladies don't take drugs. So I lay in bed thinking that surely the menstrual cramps would go away, since it was inappropriate for them to be there in the first place.

In the jargon of my profession, I was engaging in "denial," which, as the saying goes, is not just a river in Egypt. My due date was in August, and going into labor in June was unthinkable. So I fell back asleep with my menstrual cramps, only to be awakened minutes later by something gushing out of me that I took to be blood, which meant I would be dead in a matter of minutes since there was no way to get to the hospital fast enough to save my life.

I pounded Steve awake, and he flew out of bed to switch on the light. We saw, to our most incredible relief, that whatever poured out of me was definitely not blood, because it was colorless. While we were examining the wet sheet, I happened to mention to Steve that I was having menstrual cramps, of all things. He suggested instead that I was in labor, that my water had broken, and, yes, it was early, but it was happening, and that's why the bed was soaked.

I refused to accept this reality. It was not true because it was not time. Obviously the baby had kicked my bladder and knocked all the pee out of me, because I had recently heard of this very thing happening to some extremely pregnant person while she was grocery shopping. So I crouched on the bed on all fours, put my nose to the wet sheet, and insisted that Steve get down and sniff it with me. I was quite positive that I detected a definite urinelike odor.

Carol Burnett says that comedy is tragedy plus time. If I had been a fly on the wall, I would have observed a scene of great hilarity: the two of us crouched like dogs on our bed, noses to the sheet, coming up for air only long enough to fight with each other about whether we were, or were not, smelling pee. We called the doctor, who said he would meet us at the hospital right away.

Standing under the moon, outside the hospital door, all fear left me. In its place I felt the most ineffable sadness I've ever known. I turned to Steve and said, "I am so sorry." He hugged me and said that he loved me and that nothing was my fault, but I knew it was. I knew I had just committed the biggest screwup in the world. The stakes had never been so high, and I couldn't even get pregnancy right.

Labor is a well-named, all-consuming experience. When it was determined that I could go ahead with natural childbirth, I was entirely immersed in getting through it. My emotions got put aside, like an athlete competing in a major event. My obstetrician said that a helicopter would be available to fly the baby to the intensive care unit at the medical center in Kansas City, if need be. Everyone was predicting a tiny premature infant of, say, four pounds. I imagined one even smaller because, as I lay on my back and looked down, I didn't even look pregnant anymore.

There was nothing I could do but have this baby. I was taken over by the pure physicality of the event, and now everything went by the book. Soon I was being wheeled from a small dark room into a large room flooded with sunlight. I remember my body pushing for me, how struck I was with the mammalian nature of it all, and then out slid the most beautiful baby that you could ever imagine seeing in your entire life. The most beautiful *big* baby.

I didn't trust my eyes. It occurred to me that maybe he was only the size of a hamster but that, in my psychotic denial, my mind was blowing him up into a normal-sized baby. So I held my breath and waited for someone to speak. And then my doctor said, "He's *big*!" and someone else said, "Well, look at this perfect baby boy!"

Steve was beside himself with joy, and if I have ever in my life known total happiness it was then.

Matthew Rubin Lerner was twenty inches long and weighed 7 pounds, 4 ounces. He showed some signs of prematurity (three years later, his brother Ben weighed in at 9 pounds, 13 ounces), but he was not nearly as early as we had all calculated. Then he was taken away, and the next thing I heard was that he scored 9 out of 10 on his Apgar test. I didn't know what this meant, but figuring that it was like getting an A- on his first exam, I was filled with pride that he was already distinguishing himself in some academic sense while still leaving room for improvement.

My first pregnancy taught me the basics about motherhood. I learned that we are not in control of what happens to our children, that this fact needn't stop us from feeling totally guilty and responsible, that matters of life and death turn on a dime, and that most of what we worry about doesn't happen (although bad things happen that we fail to anticipate). These are the essential lessons of motherhood that were repeated again and again throughout my child-raising experience, and the universe taught them to me right up front.

BEYOND THE PURSUIT OF HAPPINESS

A friend and I are discussing a magazine survey concluding that couples without children lead happier lives. "Why report on the obvious?" my friend quips. "Of course couples without children are happier. There is layer upon layer of their emotional lives that they will never tap into. Ignorance is bliss."

I have a somewhat difference response. "No one can measure

happiness," I say. "And furthermore, the focus on 'happiness' somehow misses the point."

Americans have a constitutional right to the pursuit of happiness, but this guarantee has always struck me as absurd. I once heard novelist Isabel Allende comment that we would be better off to have a constitutional right to pursue widsom. Children are a definite gamble, as far as happiness goes, although they will bring you moments of indescribable joy.

Children are never easy, so don't bring them into the world or adopt them to bolster your happiness. And don't have them if your life's purpose is to dwell in complete stillness, serenity, and simplicity; or if you have a great dread of being interrupted; or if you are on a particular life path that demands your full attention and devotion. Also keep in mind that children are not a "solution." As Anne Lamott reminds us, there is no problem for which children are the solution.

To opt for kids is to opt for chaos, complexity, turbulence, and truth. Kids will make you love them in a way you never thought possible. They will also confront you with all the painful and unsavory emotions that humans put so much energy into trying to avoid. Children will teach you about *yourself* and about what it's like not to be up to the demands of the most important responsibility you'll ever have. They'll teach you that you are capable of deep compassion, and also that you are definitely not the nice, calm, competent, clear-thinking, highly evolved person you fancied yourself to be before you became a mother.

Your children will call on you to grow up. You will have the opportunity to achieve a more complex and textured view of your own mother. Your marriage, if it lasts, will be both deepened and strained. And whether you stay married or get divorced, the stakes are so much higher for how you navigate your part in the relationship with your child's father.

In every respect, children raise the stakes. Or as novelist Mona Simpson puts it, children *are* the stakes. She writes, "My marriage, my death, my failures or successes, my daily kindnesses or meannesses, all mean more, because they will be felt by a person other than myself as central, determining."

I also think that kids are the best teachers of life's most profound spiritual lessons: that pain and suffering are as much a part of life as happiness and joy; that change and impermanence are all we can count on for sure; that we don't really run the show; and that if we can't find the maturity to surrender to these difficult truths, we'll always be unhappy that our lives—and our children's—aren't turning out the way we expected or planned. Life doesn't go the way we expect or plan, and nobody's perfect, not ourselves or our children. Or as Elisabeth Kübler-Ross put it, "I'm not okay, you're not okay, and *that's* okay." The miracle is that your children will love you with all your imperfections if you can do the same for them.

Anger and Tenderness

Adrienne Rich

In 1976, Adrienne Rich, the distinguished poet and feminist thinker, published her pioneering work Of Woman Born, *in which she broke the silence surrounding the actual, lived experience of motherhood. A blend of memoir and cultural criticism, her book is provocative, painful, and insightful. Her writing is dense; she packs tremendous emotional weight into each sentence. Decades later, her words are still disarming, raw, and powerful. Get ready. From the first sentence of this excerpt, Rich breaks taboos, giving voice to formerly unspeakable truths.*

∼

Entry from my journal, November 1960

My children cause me the most exquisite suffering of which I have any experience. It is the suffering of ambivalence: the murderous alternation between bitter resentment and raw-edged nerves, and blissful gratification and tenderness. Sometimes I seem to myself, in my feelings toward these tiny guiltless beings, a monster of selfishness and intolerance. Their voices wear away at my

nerves, their constant needs, above all their need for simplicity and patience, fill me with despair at my own failures, despair too at my fate, which is to serve a function
for which I was not fitted. And I am weak sometimes
from held-in rage. There are times when I feel only death
will free us from one another, when I envy the barren
woman who has the luxury of her regrets but lives a life
of privacy and freedom.

And yet at other times I am melted with the sense of
their helpless, charming, and quite irresistible beauty—
their ability to go on loving and trusting—their staunch-
ness and decency and unselfconsciousness. *I love them.*
But it's in the enormity and inevitability of this love that
the sufferings lie.

April 1961

A blissful love for my children engulfs me from time to
time and seems almost to suffice—the aesthetic pleasure
I have in these little, changing creatures, the sense of
being loved, however dependently, the sense too that I'm
not an utterly unnatural and shrewish mother—much
though I am!

May 1965

To suffer with and for and against a child—maternally,
egotistically, neurotically, sometimes with a sense of
helplessness, sometimes with the illusion of learning wisdom—but always, everywhere, in body and soul, *with*
that child—because that child is a piece of oneself.

To be caught up in waves of love and hate, jealousy
even of the child's childhood; hope and fear for its ma-

turity; longing to be free of responsibility, tied by every fibre of one's being.

That curious primitive reaction of protectiveness, the beast defending her cub, when anyone attacks or criticizes him—And yet no one more hard on him than I!

September 1965

Degradation of anger. Anger at a child. How shall I learn to absorb the violence and make explicit only the caring? Exhaustion of anger. Victory of will, too dearly bought— far too dearly!

March 1966

Perhaps one is a monster—an anti-woman—something driven and without recourse to the normal and appealing consolations of love, motherhood, joy in others . . .

Unexamined assumptions: First, that a "natural" mother is a person without further identity, one who can find her chief gratification in being all day with small children, living at a pace tuned to theirs; that the isolation of mothers and children together in the home must be taken for granted; that maternal love is, and should be, quite literally selfless; that children and mothers are the "causes" of each others' suffering. I was haunted by the stereotype of the mother whose love is "unconditional"; and by the visual and literary images of motherhood as a single-minded identity. If I knew parts of myself existed that would never cohere to those images, weren't those parts then abnormal, monstrous? And—as my eldest son, now aged twenty-one, remarked on reading the above passages: "You seemed to feel you ought to love us all the time. But there *is* no human relationship where you love the person at every moment." Yes, I tried to explain to him, but women—above all, mothers—have been supposed to love that way.

From the fifties and early sixties, I remember a cycle. It began when I had picked up a book or began trying to write a letter, or even found myself on the telephone with someone toward whom my voice betrayed eagerness, a rush of sympathetic energy. The child (or children) might be absorbed in busyness, in his own dreamworld; but as soon as he felt me gliding into a world which did not include him, he would come to pull at my hand, ask for help, punch at the typewriter keys. And I would feel his wants at such a moment as fraudulent, as an attempt moreover to defraud me of living even for fifteen minutes as myself. My anger would rise; I would feel the futility of any attempt to salvage myself, and also the inequality between us: my needs always balanced against those of a child, and always losing. I could love so much better, I told myself, after even a quarter-hour of selfishness, of peace, of detachment from my children. A few minutes! But it was as if an invisible thread would pull taut between us and break, to the child's sense of inconsolable abandonment, if I moved—not even physically, but in spirit—into a realm beyond our tightly circumscribed life together. It was as if my placenta had begun to refuse him oxygen. Like so many women, I waited with impatience for the moment when their father would return from work, when for an hour or two at least the circle drawn around mother and children would grow looser, the intensity between us slacken, because there was another adult in the house.

Once in a while someone used to ask me, "Don't you ever write poems about your children?" The male poets of my generation did write poems about their children—especially their daughters. For me, poetry was where I lived as no-one's mother, where I existed as myself.

The bad and the good moments are inseparable for me. I recall the times when, suckling each of my children, I saw his eyes open full to mine, and realized each of us was fastened to the other, not only by mouth and breast, but through our mutual gaze: the depth, calm, passion, of that dark blue, maturely focused look. I recall the physical pleasure of having my full breast suckled at a time when I had no other physical pleasure in the world except the guilt-ridden pleasure of addictive eating. I remember early the sense of conflict, of a battleground none of us had chosen, of being an observer who, like it or not, was also an actor in an endless contest of wills. This was what it meant to me to have three children under the age of seven. But I recall too each child's individual body, his slenderness, wiriness, softness, grace, the beauty of little boys who have not been taught that the male body must be rigid. I remember moments of peace when for some reason it was possible to go to the bathroom alone. I remember being uprooted from already meager sleep to answer a childish nightmare, pull up a blanket, warm a consoling bottle, lead a half-asleep child to the toilet. I remember going back to bed starkly awake, brittle with anger, knowing that my broken sleep would make next day a hell, that there would be more nightmares, more need for consolation, because out of my weariness I would rage at those children for no reason they could understand. I remember thinking I would never dream again (the unconscious of the young mother—where does it entrust its messages, when dream-sleep is denied her for years?).

For many years I shrank from looking back on the first decade of my children's lives. In snapshots of the period I see a smiling young woman, in maternity clothes or bent over a half-naked baby;

gradually she stops smiling, wears a distant, half-melancholy look, as if she were listening for something. In time my sons grew older, I began changing my own life, we began to talk to each other as equals. Together we lived through my leaving the marriage, and through their father's suicide. We became survivors, four distinct people with strong bonds connecting us. Because I always tried to tell them the truth, because their every new independence meant new freedom for me, because we trusted each other even when we wanted different things, they became, at a fairly young age, self-reliant and open to the unfamiliar. Something told me that if they had survived my angers, my self-reproaches, and still trusted my love and each others', they were strong. Their lives have not been, will not be, easy; but their very existences seem a gift to me, their vitality, humor, intelligence, gentleness, love of life, their vitality, humor, intelligence, gentleness, love of life, their separate life-currents which here and there stream into my own. I don't know how we made it from their embattled childhood and my embattled motherhood into a mutual recognition of ourselves and each other. Probably that mutual recognition, overlaid by social and traditional circumstance, was always there, from the first gaze between the mother and the infant at the breast.

Giving Birth to Ambivalence

Andrea J. Buchanan

This is one of my favorite pieces of writing on motherhood to come out in recent years. Buchanan is disarmingly honest—I think many mothers will identify with her—and she beautifully conveys the way our hopes and optimism can collide with reality. At the same time, this piece is tremendously life-affirming and encouraging.

~

*T*HE FIRST THING I CAN REMEMBER thinking when they handed me my daughter seconds after her birth was "Who is this little stranger?" She didn't look like me, she didn't look like my husband; she was a tiny, perfectly formed human being, and even though I saw her completely round head, her delicate fingers, her long toes, and her calm eyes, I couldn't connect this little person with the faceless kicks and jabs I had felt inside me for so many months. I knew enough to expect that my delivery would not be the stuff of *A Baby Story*, all blurred-out yucky parts and love-at-first-sight happiness. I was still surprised to discover that my first emotion was not the intense love I'd heard described but, instead, a sense of overwhelming responsibility.

People said to me when I was pregnant, "Oh, your life is going to change!" as if they were not stating the obvious. My life had already changed—I was pregnant—and when it came time for the baby to be born my life would change again. What they didn't tell me was exactly how it would change or the ways in which it would change me. I knew to expect sleepless nights; I knew to expect crying; I knew to expect exhaustion; I even knew to expect joy. I didn't know to expect ambivalence. I didn't know to expect doubt.

For the two days I spent in the hospital recovering from my delivery, I was on an adrenaline high. We had too many visitors to count, and I welcomed them all as they cooed over our new daughter. The baby and my husband stayed in the room with me, and a wonderful staff of nurses nursed us through our first tentative days as parents.

Things changed when we got home. I hadn't gotten more than four hours' sleep in the two days I was in the hospital. I was so sore it felt like I'd been run over by a truck. And the inevitable hormonal roller-coaster had begun as my body did its job of adjusting to no longer supporting another life. I became extremely weepy and cried over everything and nothing—catching a glimpse of my non-pregnant body in the mirror; getting out of bed the way I used to when I was pregnant and then suddenly realizing that I no longer had a huge, weighty belly to maneuver around; putting on a pair of sweatpants I wore for the last month of my pregnancy and being shocked when the waistband snapped back to fit so loosely on my stomach. I missed being pregnant, and I cried all the time unless I had my baby with me. I held her the whole time I was awake and slept with her in my arms. Nearly every time I dozed off I dreamt she was still inside me, kicking, only to wake up and find myself cradling her next to me.

But I had read the books, I knew what to expect about those first few weeks. It was normal for me to have "baby blues." I'd get past it. And so when people said to me, "Isn't motherhood just the best thing ever?" and "Do you just spend all day kissing those little baby toes?" I said what I was supposed to say. Which was that I loved every minute of it, that I didn't mind one bit being sleep-deprived, that being a mom was the greatest thing in the world. I figured eventually I really would mean those things.

I jumped right back into my job. Since I was working from home, I figured, how hard could it be? I found out soon enough. I learned the hard way not to underestimate the stress of trying to negotiate being both a new mom and a good employee. Immediately and constantly, I felt torn by the demand of deadlines: who comes first, the client or the baby? Faxing those galleys or changing that dirty diaper? Either choice meant failing one or the other.

I began to have insomnia. Once my daughter woke up in the night I would be up for hours, lying awake and beating myself up for not being better at this mothering thing. Why did it seem so easy for everyone else? Why was it so difficult for me? I had been used to doing difficult things, but I had been used to succeeding at them. I never imagined it would take a little six-pound baby to bring me to my knees.

I felt helpless, I felt overwhelmed. I wished things were back to the way they were when I was pregnant, when being a good mother basically just meant remembering to take my prenatal vi-tamins. Things were so much easier when we shared a body: I could be a mother without knowing how to mother, I could take care of my baby without having to worry if what I was doing was right or wrong. I didn't realize how terrified I was of failing at mothering, failing my daughter, until one night when my husband asked me for the 150th time that hour, "Do you think she's okay, do you think she's still breathing?" And I thought: what a relief it would be if she weren't okay, what a relief it would be if she were gone.

It was a horrible moment, a horrible thought, and I instantly felt like a horrible mother for thinking it. I felt a sickening kinship with those mothers and fathers you hear about on the news and read about in the papers, parents or caregivers who snap, who shake or hit or leave or hurt their babies in a fit of insanity or desperation or plain old sleep deprivation. Before I was a parent I would think, "How could anyone hurt her own child?" But here I was with a good-natured baby, a supportive husband, a nice apartment with a washer and dryer—here I was with seemingly everything made easy for me, and yet I still felt awed in the face of responsibility, I still felt like I couldn't handle it.

I had terrible fantasies. Driving home from the grandparents' house, I would half imagine/half hope that my husband would swerve our car into the huge semi next to us. I would, in a fit of desperation, envision the horrible crash that would ensue and experience for a moment the fleeting sensation of relief that all of this— this being a mother—would be over.

One night when I couldn't sleep, I lay awake planning in detail my escape: I would pack a small overnight bag and slip out at 3:00 A.M. No note, no message. I'd just leave. I would go to the ATM and take out as much cash as I could. I would walk over to the bus station at 11th and Market and take the bus that went farthest. I couldn't go to New York, nor New Jersey nor Boston nor California; those were all places my husband would think to look for me. I would go somewhere nameless, faceless, some small town in the middle of some unheard-of place, where I could have no identity and just start over. I would get a job waitressing. I would live in a motel. I would do whatever it took to make some money to live on, and I would sleep all night. My time would finally be my own. I drifted off to sleep, eventually, lulled by the fantasy of escape. In the morning, I remembered my midnight plan and told my husband, laughing at how ridiculous it sounded in the light of day. I expected him to be a little horrified, but when I finished telling him my secret scheme, all he asked was "Were you going to go by yourself or were you going to take the baby?"

I kept telling myself, everyone does this, everyone survives it. Women give birth and become mothers every day, right here in this city, in cities I've never heard of, in cities around the world. I was one of an endless succession of women going through that profound physical and emotional transformation every day. The thought was both humbling and encouraging. How did mothers mother back in the fourteenth century? Did they talk about feeling helpless, did they talk about feeling lost? How about Victorian mothers? Did they suffer the indignities of their postpartum bodies in private, were they entirely alone in their experiences? And what of mothers in underdeveloped countries, mothers living on the edge of poverty in our own country? Women have been becoming mothers since the beginning of human history, I kept reminding myself. If they can do it, I can too.

Eventually I cut my work hours to part-time. Eventually I found other new mothers forging their way through similarly emotional territory. Eventually I began to doubt myself less and trust myself more. Eventually I began to mean it when I'd say sure, yes, being a mom is the best thing ever. My insomnia gradually disappeared and my baby started getting into a routine, napping in the day and sleeping for extended stretches through the night. I felt more like my old self, less like I had crossed over into some strange place I was not prepared to enter.

One day when my daughter was about four months old, I was in the park with her. She was sleeping, I was reading. I was feeling good, feeling happy, feeling confident. A family walked by us, a tall man holding hands with a little girl who looked to be about eight, a woman walking just behind them. They stopped and looked at my sleeping baby and we had the standard conversation—how old she was, how much she weighed, how much she slept. I smiled and they smiled back and they went on their way. A few moments later, I was surprised to see the woman hesitate and turn around to come back to where I was.

"Do you see that little girl there?" she asked me, pointing to the girl I had assumed was her daughter. "That's my granddaughter. That man holding her hand is my little baby. He's thirty-eight now, but he's still my baby." I told her she didn't look old enough to have a thirty-eight year old baby, that I had thought she was the little girl's mother. She shook her head and smiled at me. Suddenly it looked as though she had tears in her eyes, and she reached down and squeezed my hand. "I just wanted to tell you," she whispered, "it gets better. It gets so much better from here."

I think about her a lot, especially when things are better. How brave of her to tell me, how thoughtful of her to sense I needed to hear that. She couldn't know, of course, how badly I needed to have someone reassure me that I was a good mother, that it's tough at first for everyone, and for all she knew I could have been offended by what might have seemed an assumption of my incapability. But she told me, and I often tell the story of her telling me to other new mothers I meet.

"It gets so much better from here," she told me.

She was right.

My Daughter at Fourteen

Carolyn Magner Mason

In the early years of parenting, we mothers are like gods to our children, all-powerful, all-knowing, the ultimate source of comfort. When my boys were babies, they each went through a phase when they would burst into tears if I so much as left their field of vision. Still, I've always tried to remember that it wouldn't last. I'd imagine them as teenagers, embarrassed to be seen with me in public, their bedroom doors festooned with police tape and a sign saying "KEEP OUT!" In this essay, Mason writes about the downward trajectory of "Mom" as our children grow.

∼

SHE WAS FOUR YEARS OLD and mad as hell. It was something I did or didn't do and fury creased her face and clenched her hands into tight little fists. I gently asked her what was wrong, and she took a deep breath, her chest caving in and her eyes sending icy spikes at my heart. Finally she spoke: "I've never liked you."

"What? Never? In four whole years on planet earth, you've never liked me?"

"That's right," she said, and stalked out of the room.

Ten years later, we are driving to an out-of-town mall when she casually mentions that her friends don't like me. "Yeah, they like Paige's mom and they like Amanda's mom, but they don't like you." She goes back to sipping her Mountain Dew.

"So, uh, why don't they like me?" I ask, carefully keeping my voice neutral.

"I don't know, you just aren't fun."

"Oh, that explains it," I say.

In between four and fourteen I had a great run. For a brief decade, I was the most popular one in the family. Everyone wanted to sit next to me, sleep beside me, and hold my hand in church. Everyone wanted my opinion on everything from their hair to their socks. I was the expert nurse, entertainer, and homework helper. There was nothing I wasn't good at and there was no outfit that didn't make me look like a movie star. I wasn't just fun, I was downright hilarious.

Then, one day, my daughter turned fourteen. I went to bed a goddess and awoke a slug. My tiara didn't just slip over my eyes; it crashed to the ground and shattered into a million sharp pieces.

Somehow it doesn't bother me. Not that I wouldn't prefer goddess stature, but I was always waiting for the crash and could never really enjoy the adulation like I should have. Every time she gasped, "Oh Mama, you are the prettiest mom in the fourth grade," I would stand there, tiara in hand, unable to soak it in. If it's too good to be true, then it is.

I confess: I thought I might escape. There were whole years when I thought I was not going to be the kind of mother to have issues with my teenage daughters. I'm too cool, too hip, too understanding to ever fall for something as banal as not getting along with my teenager. But the story of the furious four-year-old was always there, foretelling the future.

Luckily, I was never one of those insufferable mothers who proclaimed from their minivan, "My child will never . . ." Those of us in the trenches are bound by the knowledge that not only might they, but they probably will. We hope, we pray, we cross our fingers, but we never say never. And I'm not mean enough to point out to my daughter that Amanda and Paige don't think their mothers are "all that," either.

I pop out her Dave Matthews CD and insert my Enya. She doesn't say anything, perhaps feeling a little ashamed of knifing the one with the credit card and driver's license. We continue in silence.

My own mother watches my relationship with my daughter unfold with amusement. I tell her I'm not taking this personally. She is nice to not remind me of how sullen, distant, moody, and ungrateful I was at fourteen. She keeps telling me to lighten up, chill out, relax, and enjoy the good times. There is something very comforting about getting teenage-girl advice from one's own mother, a prisoner of war who returned, maybe not unscathed but undaunted. I figure if she can take a chill pill, so can I.

She lets me wax on about how my daughter has incredible pressures I never had. My daughter's world is faster, more intense, more graphic than mine was. I swing wildly between the philosophies of roots and wings. Do I protect her or just try to be there to pick up the pieces? Am I her fun mother-friend or just her mother? Do I stick to my un-fun guns or do I throw up my hands and say, "Do what you want to do!"?

I ask one last question after we pull up in front of Old Navy.

"What kind of daughter do you hope you'll have?"

She looks a little frightened. She is about to get her low-rise corduroys and doesn't want to give the wrong answer so close to the cash register.

"Uh, I hope she's like me, only nicer," she says, eyebrows raised, hoping it will work.

It works for me. Let's shop.

The Way I Dreamed It

Ariel Gore

In the tradition of Adrienne Rich, Ariel Gore expresses her experience with boldness and honesty—though her writing is far more informal, and also a lot funnier. She is a self-described "hip mama," young, irreverent, tattooed, in touch with today's youth culture. Here she reflects on the surprising difficulty of dealing with her own daughter's adolescent rebellion.

~

ERE'S THE WAY I DREAMED IT: My daughter and I would glide into her teen years, our tight bond intact. With the steady stream of grown-up eccentrics wandering in and out of our lives, she'd have no reason to rebel. She'd ease into whatever identity she wanted to project—punk or goth, hippie or politico. My own musical tastes would keep up with the times, and together we'd rock out to the top forty on the alternative charts. Since I am a sex-positive and easygoing mama, my daughter would freely ask me about anything she had on her mind. I'd tell her the truth, and she'd follow my advice, because even though we'd get along like comrades, we *wouldn't* be best friends: We'd be mother and daughter—I wisely pointing her in the right direction, she proudly on her way. Lovely and boring.

And why shouldn't I have imagined it that way? When my kid was in elementary school, she was a smaller, cooler version of me. Sure, life changed and moved forward with each passing year . . . a new privilege here, a childhood toy tossed aside there. Nothing drastic. My daughter was slowly moving toward self-sufficiency. By age eleven she could get herself to school and back. She could fix a simple meal and put together a complex outfit. She could design a dream home and recognize a Georgia O'Keeffe painting. With some prompting, she could remember to wear a coat when it was cold, remember her homework assignments, and remember what time she had to be at tae kwon do.

I taught her my politics, my values, my fashion sense. And she was making those things her own. We went to protests together. We traveled the world. We thought the same things were beautiful, the same things scary. I was a zinester, she was a zinester. I was a writer, she was an artist. I wore black, she wore black. She was, essentially, Mini-Me—custom raised for my lifestyle.

And then one day she woke up, put on a pink shirt, and announced her plan to try out for the cheerleading team.

My eyes widened. I took a deep breath.

She said, "Mom, I know you might not support my decision."

"That's right," I nodded, then exhaled. "But I support *you.*"

She bit her lip. "I'll raise all the money for my uniform."

"Yes, you will. And I'll be there at all the games."

She'd warned me, when she was twelve: *"Having a baby or a kid might be hard, but you get to raise it in your world. When you're raising a teenager, you have to go into their world."* Into her world. But how?

Sometimes in a crowd, when I see her out of the corner of my eye, or from afar, I don't even recognize her. In my mind's eye, I just register a teenager or young woman—fifteen or twenty-two. She's got long brown hair with blonde streaks in it. She wears a fuzzy white sweater, a heart on a chain around her neck, black boot-cut jeans, Adidas. She's about my height—on the short side for a grownup, but too tall to be a kid. She's slender, composed, blasé. She's cool in a princessy sort of way. The kind of girl who probably wouldn't have spoken to me when I was that age.

I'm nearsighted. And anyway, she doesn't make eye contact until she has to. Embarrassed to see me. Embarrassed to be seen with me. But she comes closer. I do a double take. When I realize who she is, she suddenly appears smaller. Younger. She becomes a child—ten or twelve.

I refocus. This girl-woman is my baby. I see her infant-smooth skin under the pale face powder. Yet here she stands, thirteen years old, strong, vulnerable.

When I pick her up from school, I sometimes forget to wear my shoes. When she fails to look both ways before crossing the street, I scold her like she's five. I correct her friends when they say that Mexicans speak "Mexican." I tell her boyfriends they have to come in through the front door instead of using the back window. I shout at neighborhood kids not to threaten each other with big sticks.

She wants me to stop it. *Into her world.* But I hardly recognize her there.

At home, when no one is looking, she comes back into my world—if only for a few minutes or hours. She wants to talk about the way things were when *I* was a kid. Or when she was a baby. She wants me to brush her hair. She wants me to tuck her in. She wants me to lie with her as she falls asleep.

"Mama? Don't leave me."

I lie down, cuddle up next to her.

"Mama? I can't get to sleep."

I tell her to think about the Sierras, about a lake she knows well, to close her eyes and picture the whole scene.

"Mama?" she sits up a little. "The kids at school are smoking dope."

"Huh?"

"How old do you think kids should be before they smoke dope?"

It takes me a minute to readjust to the turn the conversation has taken, to the turns the years have taken. I clear my throat. "They probably shouldn't smoke it at all. But if they have to smoke it, they should wait until high school. I mean, no offense to your age group, but most of your friends can't get to Noah's and back with a half-dozen garlic bagels without getting distracted. You don't have that many brain cells to spare."

She laughs. "You have to say that because you're the *mom*."

"True enough," I admit. "I'm biased. But I'll talk to you about anything you want to talk about. If you ever feel uncomfortable asking me things, Moe and Krystee and Inga are other good people to talk to, OK?"

"OK," she yawns.

She looks so little. Sleepy-eyed. Needy.

In the morning she'll apply a thick layer of face powder and ask me to drop her off a block away from school so as not to be seen with me.

Into her world.

Here's a card my daughter, Maia, wrote for a friend's thirteenth birthday:

> Sup Sammi Girl!
> It's the big 1-3! Know what that means? You're a teen! Now's your opportunity to: Get wild/crazy and blame it on your hormones, sneak out with all your girls in your parents' brand new BMW and still blend in, and last but not least, have a chance to be tak'n seriously (just playin'!!), and even though it's just the beginning of your "teenhood," it's only seven years. So, you bring the map, I'll bring the shot glasses and let's paaaty!!
> (I'm just joking, Mr. & Mrs. Jackson!)
>
> > Lotsa Luv,
> > Maia

The big 1-3.

Poor Mr. and Mrs. Jackson.

Poor me!

Our kids' teen years constitute the most-feared period of a parent's life. From the time they're babies, we're warned about the horrors to come. "Just you wait," we're told. As if our new-parent culture shock and suddenly sleepless nights are nothing compared to What Will Come.

We dread adolescence. We deny it will happen to *our* family. *I'll be a different kind of parent,* we tell ourselves. We won't give our teens anything to rebel against. The worlds we've raised them in— our worlds—are beautiful, exciting, diverse. Our children won't *need* to break away.

We fear adolescence for a lot of reasons. We worry about our kids' safety. We don't want to lose control. We don't want our kids to experience pain—and we remember so much pain from those years in our own lives. It's only human that as parents, we want to be loved and accepted. We don't want our every comment picked apart and found lacking, thrown back in our faces. We don't want to go to football games or enter worlds outside our comfort zones. And, frankly, we don't want to get old. If our children are young adults, what does that make *us?* Our culture teaches us to be scared of teenagers, but also to glorify the teen years. The adolescent appearance is considered the height of beauty and sex appeal. Teen culture—when it's not depicted as depraved and self-destructive—is seen as incomparably cool, revolutionary, *fun.* John Cougar Mellencamp told us it would be downhill as soon as we let go of age sixteen. And so we hung on. We believed him. If our kids are now approaching Jack and Diane's age, how *totally* long gone are all the thrills of our own lives?

We're warned that the parent-teen relationship, for its part, is intrinsically adversarial. Our kids will be raging wild against us and hating everything about us down to the way we brush our teeth. They'll be making life choices so far from anything we ever would have chosen for them that we'll be hating *them,* too. Defiant monsters.

It's true that our kids will not be us. But the real and lived separation of our worlds, it turns out, is far from anything that old songs or conventional wisdom ever taught us. Teenage kids are complex, fragile, feisty. The life phase they're going through is full of optimism, curiosity, tribulation, and unexpected twists. Becoming the parent of a teenager is just as myth-shattering, mind-blowing, heartbreaking, and awesome as becoming a parent in the first place. But it doesn't have to be the end of all that was good and loving about our families.

It's also true that we're not sixteen anymore. But John Cougar Mellencamp was full of it. For most of us, hanging on to sixteen would be hanging on to our pre-experienced, pre-initiated, pre-intuitive selves. The road to maturity is a rough one. We don't want to admit that we've been through it. Our scars show. And judging from the wealth of the makers of Botox, antiwrinkle cream, and hair dye, most of us are less than proud of our scars. Still, I dare you to find one grownup who honestly wants to go back to being who they were then. We mourn our youthful appearance, but we cherish our inner development. We want to be sixteen again, but not without knowing what we know now. We want our kids to be sixteen, too—aren't they beautiful?—but we want them to carry *our* grown-up wisdom and values into *their* world. This cannot be. Our kids will carry some of our wisdom—that's what evolution's all about—but only some of it. They'll trash some of our values, too—that's also what evolution is about.

Adolescence includes some serious lows, but many of those lows are necessary rites of passage. Our kids are beginning to take control of their own destinies, and they're going to have to do it in their own ways.

As parents, then, how do we deal? What are our responsibilities at this point? I figure our tasks are eightfold: to be ourselves, to pay attention; to speak our truths and do our best to communicate whatever wisdom we have; to cultivate compassion about the fact that these years can be extremely difficult for both ourselves and our kids; to be fierce about the things that truly matter to us; to lighten up and let go of the things that are trivial; to accept that all we can do sometimes is pray for the best outcome; and, yes, to let go of sixteen ourselves.

One Week until College

Sandi Kahn Shelton

This selection gets to me every time I read it. Mothering is so intense, filled with ups and downs, and sometimes its daily, unrelenting demands feel like too much. But then, one day, the kids move out. That's it; they're gone. There's a saying that when you're raising children, the days are long but the years are short. When the time comes for them to leave home, how will it be to let go and say goodbye?

~

*M*Y DAUGHTER, ALLIE, IS leaving for college in one week. What this means for today—when it's still not time to say good-bye—is that it's impossible to make a path through her room. The floor is cluttered with bags from Filene's and J. Crew: They're filled with extra-long sheets for her dormitory bed, fleece blankets still in their wrappers, thick dark blue towels, washcloths, new pairs of jeans and sweaters, baskets of shampoo and loofahs.

She won't talk about going.

I say, "I'm going to miss you," and she gives me one of her looks and finds a reason to leave the room.

Another time I say, in a voice so friendly it surprises even me: "Do you think you'll take down your posters and pictures and take them with you, or will you get new ones at college?"

She answers, in a voice filled with annoyance, "How should I know?"

I was also eighteen when I left home in 1970, but instead of moving to college, I was leaving to live with my boyfriend. I had been angry with my mother for months before I left. I flung my belongings in cardboard boxes, taking everything with me because I was never, never coming back home again. My mother stood in the doorway, her arms folded, and said I was making a huge mistake. "If what you're hoping for is marriage, this isn't the way to get it," she said. "He'll just live with you and then toss you away when something better comes along. I know that type." "I'm not looking for marriage," I responded. "I'm just looking for a chance to get out of here."

My daughter is off with friends most of the time. Yesterday was the last day she'd have until Christmas with her friend Katharine, whom she'd known since kindergarten. Soon, very soon, it will be her last day with Sarah, Claire, Heather, and Lauren.

And then it will be her last day with me. My friend Karen told me, "The August before I left for college, I screamed at my mother the whole month. Be prepared."

We in our forties have mostly learned to forgive our mothers for the crimes they committed in raising us. We have paid therapists thousands of dollars and spent endless hours talking with friends, going over and over the mistakes that were our legacy, and we have figured out how not to make the same errors with our daughters. We know just what kind of support girls need.

In the cooperative day-care center my daughter attended, the young mothers sat down with storybooks and patiently crossed out all sexist references. We told them they could be anything they wanted to be. We said, "Don't let the boys win. You're as big and strong and capable as they are!"

So they simply can't be as angry with us as we were with our own mothers.

Yet I stand here in the kitchen, watching my daughter make a glass of iced tea. Her face, once so open and trusting, is closed to me. I struggle to think of something to say to her, something friendly and warm. I would like her to know that I admire her, that I am excited about the college she has chosen, that I know the adventure of her life is just about to get started, and that I am so proud of how she's handling everything.

But here's the thing: The look on her face is so mad that I think she might slug me if I open my mouth.

I can't think what I have done. One night not long ago—after a particularly long period of silence between us—I asked what I might have done or said to make her angry with me. I felt foolish saying it. My own mother, who ruled the house with such authoritative majesty, would never have deigned to find out what I thought or felt about anything she did. But there I was, obviously having offended my daughter, and I wanted to know. I felt vulnerable asking the question, but it was important.

She sighed, as though this question were more evidence of a problem so vast and fundamental that it could never be explained, and she said, "Mom, you haven't done anything. It's fine."

It *is* fine. It's just distant, that's all. May I tell you how close we once were? When she was two years old, my husband and I divorced—one of those modern, amiable divorces that was just great for all parties involved, except that I had to quit my part-time job and take a full-time position. When I would come to the day-care center to pick Allie up after work, she and I would sit on the reading mattress together, and she would nurse. For a whole year after that divorce, we would sit every day at five o'clock, our eyes locked together, concentrating on and reconnecting with each other at the end of our public day. In middle school, when other mothers were already lamenting the estrangement they felt with their adolescent daughters, I hit upon what seemed the perfect solution: rescue raids. I would simply show up occasionally at the school, sign her out of class, and take her somewhere—out to lunch, off to the movies, once on a long walk on the beach. It may sound irresponsible, unsupportive of education, but it worked. It kept us close when around us other mothers and daughters were floundering. We talked about everything on those outings, outings we kept secret from the rest of the family and even from friends.

Sometimes, blow-drying her hair in the bathroom while I brushed my teeth, she'd say, "Mom, I really could use a rescue raid soon." And so I would arrange my work schedule to make one possible.

Anyone will tell you that high school is hard on the mother-daughter bond, and so it was for us, too. I'd get up with her in the early mornings to make her sandwich for school, and we'd silently drink a cup of tea together before the six-forty school bus came. But then she decided she'd rather buy her lunch at school, and she came right out and said she'd prefer to be alone in the mornings while she got ready. It was hard to concentrate on everything she needed to do with someone else standing there, she said.

We didn't have the typical fights that the media lead us to expect with teenagers: She didn't go in for tattoos and body piercings; she was mostly good about curfews; she didn't drink or do drugs.

Her friends seemed nice, and the boys she occasionally brought home were polite and acceptable.

But what happened? More and more often, I'd feel her eyes boring into me when I was living my regular life, doing my usual things: talking on the phone with friends, disciplining her younger sister, cleaning the bathroom. And the look on her face was a look of frozen disapproval, disappointment . . . even rage.

A couple of times during her senior year I went into her room at night, when the light was off but before she went to sleep. I sat on the edge of her bed and managed to find things to say that didn't enrage or disappoint her. She told me, sometimes, about problems she was having at school: a teacher who lowered her grade because she was too shy to talk in class, a boy who teased her between classes, a friend who had started smoking. Her disembodied voice, coming out of the darkness, sounded young and questioning. She listened when I said things. A few days later, I'd hear her on the phone, repeating some of the things I had said, things she had adopted for her own, and I felt glad to have been there with her that night.

I said to myself, "Somehow I can be the right kind of mother. Somehow we will find our way back to closeness again."

We haven't found our way back. And now we are having two different kinds of Augusts. I want a romantic August, where we stock up together on things she will need in her dormitory. I want to go to lunch and lean across the table toward each other, the way we've all seen mothers and daughters do, and say how much we will miss each other. I want smiles through tears, bittersweet moments of reminiscence, and the chance to offer the last little bits of wisdom I might be able to summon for her.

But she is having an August where her feelings have gone underground, where to reach over and touch her arm seems an act of war. She pulls away, eyes hard. She turns down every invitation I extend, no matter how lightly I offer them; instead of coming out with me, she lies on her bed reading Emily Dickinson until I say I have always loved Emily Dickinson, and then—but is this just a coincidence?—she closes the book.

Books I have read about surviving adolescence say that the closer your bond with your child, the more violent is the child's need to break away from you, to establish her own identity in the world. The more it will hurt, they say.

My husband says, "She's missing you so much already that she can't bear it."

A friend of mine, an editor in New York who went through a difficult adolescence with her daughter but now has become close to her again, tells me, "You're a wonderful mother. Your daughter will be back to you."

"I don't know," I say to them. I sometimes feel so angry around her that I want to go over and shake her. I want to say, "Talk to me! Either you talk to me—or you're grounded!" I can actually feel myself wanting to say that most horrible of all mother phrases: "Think of everything I've done for you. Don't you appreciate how I've suffered and struggled to give you what you need?"

I can see how the mother-daughter relationship could turn primitive and ugly. One night I go into the den and watch *Fiddler on the Roof* with my younger daughter. She's nine, and she cuddles up next to me on the couch. We weep over the daughters saying good-bye. "It's a little like Allie leaving," she says. I hug her to me ferociously, as though I could hug all daughters trying to break away. I am not unaware that I am hugging my long-ago self, standing there so furiously, glaring at my mother, unable to forgive her.

Late at night, when I'm exhausted with the effort of trying not to mind the loneliness I've felt all day around her, I am getting ready for bed. She shows up at the door of the bathroom, watches me brush my teeth in a way she doesn't approve of, and I'll be upbraided for it.

But then she says, "I want to read you something." She's holding a handbook sent by her college. "These are tips for parents," she says.

I watch her face as she reads the advice aloud. " 'Don't ask your student if she is homesick,' it says. 'She might feel bad the first few weeks, but don't let it worry you. This is a natural time of transition. Write her letters and call her a lot. Send a package of goodies. . . .' "

Her voice breaks, and she comes over to me and buries her head in my shoulder. I stroke her hair, lightly, afraid she'll bolt if I say a word. We stand there together for long moments, swaying.

I know it will be hard again. We probably won't have sentimental lunches in restaurants before she leaves, and most likely there will be a fight about something. But I am grateful to be standing in the bathroom at midnight, both of us tired and sad, toothpaste smeared on my chin, holding tight—while at the same time letting go of—this daughter who is trying to say good-bye.

Part Two

~

The Inner Work of Motherhood

Dawn

Rabbi Nancy Fuchs-Kreimer

One of the major challenges of becoming a parent is getting used to the hours. Suddenly we're on call twenty-four hours a day—and our day can start shockingly early. In this essay, Rabbi Fuchs-Kreimer explores how the early mornings we're forced to experience with our children can offer us an opportunity to reconnect with ourselves and our spirits.

~

YEARS AGO I WROTE A BOOK called *Parenting as a Spiritual Journey*. When I told people I was writing a book about the spiritual experiences of parents, many assumed that I meant the experience of giving birth. It seemed clear to them that participating in the arrival on earth of a new human being would be a "religious high." The drudgery of the next eighteen years has a less obvious connection to holiness. This essay is about both—the extraordinary, unique experience of birth and the ordinary, quotidian experience of waking up early each morning with children. Both evoke the mystery that religious people call "creation."

For many years, on Friday mornings I went with my child to

"play group." (In the interest of honesty, we should have called it "talk group" since the adults' agenda was clearly central.) One winter, we moms spent weeks on a single topic: How did other women combine children and jobs more efficiently than we? *What did they know that we did not?*

One week, Joan arrived at play group full of excitement. She had met a professional woman with three children who was publishing articles at the same rate as when she was childless. What was more, she had told Joan her secret. "All you have to do," Joan explained to a hushed and attentive audience, "is set your alarm to wake up two hours before the earliest rising child."

We were dumbfounded. It was brilliant! Why hadn't any of us thought of that? We were so desperate (and sleep deprived) that we actually believed it would work.

That night I went home and made a list of what I would do with the extra two hours. First, I would say morning blessings—something I had not done alone in years. Then, I would write in my journal. Next, I would take an aerobic walk. Finally, I would work at my computer until my daughter awoke. That night, I set the alarm, full of anticipation.

The next morning, the alarm rang. I turned it off—and promptly went back to sleep. Two hours later, my four-year-old daughter climbed into bed and woke me up, a practice she gave up just in time to turn it over to her younger sister, who has continued it to this day.

At the next play group, we checked in. The method had not worked for anyone. Then someone asked Joan who this woman was. When she told us, Susan said, "I know her! She's not even a nice person!"

Anne was exultant. "Of course not! How could she be nice? She's probably too tired!"

"Besides," Andrea pointed out, "She might get sick from so little sleep."

We all agreed that waking up too early was unhealthy at best, immoral at worst, and undeniably undoable—at least by us. We all agreed we would not wake up a minute before we had to. But once awake (admittedly, earlier than we would like), we would try to treat it as a spiritual opportunity.

What is spiritual about being up when you wish you were still asleep? For one thing, the world has been created once again. Cindy told me she had never fully grasped how beautiful morning was until her child, who had picked up some Bible stories somewhere, announced, "Look, Mom. Do you see the sky? When God created the world, it probably looked just like this morning!" This child had not heard the old Protestant hymn that begins, "Morning has broken, like the first morning." But she understood it.

Some parents find morning a good place to begin a prayer life. Morning is such a rushed and harried time, so often lacking in moments of quiet and sanctity, that it cries out for something to elevate it, to introduce thoughts beyond "Why are there never two matching socks?" Harry said, "When my baby was little, if she didn't wake up in the middle of the night, we would wake up anyway and go in just to check her breathing!" (More than one father and mother made that confession.) He went on, "It just seemed so natural to start saying the Jewish prayer for waking up—'Thank you for restoring my breath to me.' When I woke each morning, I would put on my prayer shawl and just say that one verse; it was all I had time for. My daughter would often curl up in my lap while I said it. When my daughter was six, she started sleeping later than I did, but she'd often instruct me to wake her up so she wouldn't miss the prayer."

Sometimes, perhaps most times, morning prayers are uttered in a rote fashion, and the whole business is over in a few minutes. These times are not useless. A Hasidic master, Menachem Mendel of Kotzk, was once asked, "Why does it say (in Deuteronomy 6:6) that God's words should be *al levavecha,* 'upon your heart'? Shouldn't it say that they should be *in* your heart?"

"Of course they *should* be in your heart," the rebbe replied. "But that is not always possible. At the very least, you can put them *on* your heart. They may just sit there for a very long time. But someday, your heart will crack, and if they are already on top of your heart, they can slip right in."

Ritual creates its own feedback. We hold hands with a child as the sun rises, and we sense, in a way we never did before, that the world is being reborn before our eyes. Suddenly we are in the presence of the unutterable. Believing now in the world's rebirth, we choose to make that hand-holding part of our daily lives, perhaps adding some word of prayer, perhaps creating a miniritual. Along with our child, we find a language to express what cannot be spoken. Using that language over and over, we are confirmed in our initial hunch. The world is as pregnant with meaning as the sunrise with the day.

Marsha has a childhood memory of mornings when her immigrant grandmother slept at her house. "Grandma had her own morning ritual. She would wake up early with me and take me for a walk all around the house and the yard. We would say, 'Good morning, tree! Good morning, sun! Good morning, mirror!' Sometimes we would spend twenty minutes saying good morning to our world."

Mary Lou grew up in a very religious Catholic home. Every morning, her mother would gather her family together for morning prayers. "Praying wasn't a big deal. It was like breathing. You never questioned it. I still remember what we said in the morning: 'Oh, Jesus, I offer you my prayers, works, and sufferings of this day.' I remember as a child thinking, 'I don't really do much work or suffering,' so I just moved my mouth for that part." I asked Mary Lou if she continued to say that prayer when she was the mother of ten and did not lack for work or suffering of her own. "By then I didn't have time! When I had ten children, I woke up every morning and said the shortest prayer I could—the one that I needed the most. 'Oh, God, please give me patience.' That was it."

Judaism prescribes blessings for ordinary events and blessings for extraordinary ones. The ordinary event, the daily rising of the sun, is greeted with a blessing that evokes a time when the world had just come into being: "We praise God who daily renews the works of creation." When it comes to extraordinary events, there is also a blessing, not well known among modern Jews, that mentions creation. The blessing is to be said "upon seeing lightning, comets, falling stars, vast deserts, great rivers, high mountains, experiencing a great storm or an earthquake, or seeing a strikingly clear morning after an all-night rainstorm." It reads, "We praise you God who provides us with moments reminiscent of creation."

When I first heard that blessing, shortly after the 1994 Los Angeles quake, I thought it was a wonderful way to frame what was otherwise a random, frightening, and senseless event. I was struck, however, that the authors of the blessing had not mentioned what by all counts is even more "reminiscent of creation" than an earthquake: the birth of a child. Alas, amazingly, there is no official blessing in Judaism for the moment of birth! But parents have confirmed what I already knew. Being present at the birth of a child, like witnessing the clear morning after an all-night rain, makes the whole miracle of creation more real. The ancient Polynesians also saw the connection between the arrival of a new life and the first stirrings of life itself. At the birth of each royal child, they would chant their creation myth, the Kumulipo.

There was a time when the world began. Having witnessed a birth, parents seem to find that notion a bit less implausible. "There we were in a room with three people . . . and suddenly there was one more!" said one mother. A midwife I interviewed told me, "Every time I assist a mother giving birth, I always prepare her in advance. I share with her my belief that at the instant she looks into the face of her newborn child for the first time, just for that second, she will see the face of God."

"I tell both my children," one mother said, "that God gave them a kiss the second before they were born, to send them on their journey. They like to hear that. And I believe it's true. They came out looking like they had just been kissed, at least to me." A father said, "I had read in *Spiritual Midwifery* [by Ida May Gaskin] that 'every child born is a living Buddha.' I had no idea what that meant until I saw it with my own eyes. For a minute there, it seemed like the universe paused and shifted slightly to make room for this new being, totally pure and totally wise."

One father told me about the personal imagery that summed up the birth experience for him. "There was a time in my life when I lived in a stone farmhouse in the hill country of Tuscany. The windows were just open spaces, no screens or panes, covered with heavy wooden shutters. At night, we would close the shutters. In the morning I would awaken in a room that was completely dark. I would get out of bed, walk to the window, and throw open the shutters. In one second, everything was transformed. Suddenly, the room was filled: with the sight of lush green hills, with golden light pouring in, with gentle breezes, with the smell of wildflowers, with the sound of hummingbirds. That was the way I felt in the minutes after the birth of our baby. Someone had just opened a window."

Jeffrey calls the birth of his child "the most spiritual moment of my entire life." He went on to explain: "When we first discussed having children, it was hard for me to believe that I could be a nurturing, caring father. But I had nine months to get used to the idea, to put my hand on Jane's belly and feel the baby kicking, to attend childbirth classes with Jane and read all the books. The truth is, I thought the classes were for show. I was convinced that when it came to that awesome moment when the child was born, they would lock me in the closet."

I wondered why.

"I had been in the marines in Vietnam. I saw myself as a person who had been participating in organized murder and mayhem from the age of eighteen. I had killed a ten-year-old child at close range. I didn't think I could possibly be allowed to witness a birth. But I was wrong. I was there every minute. When we had counted the fingers and toes, the baby was laid on Jane's breast to nurse and I just cried my eyes out. It was only later that it even occurred to me to ask if it was a boy or a girl.

"As far as religion goes," Jeffrey continued, "my father had been a prowar minister, and after Vietnam, the whole issue seemed settled for me once and for all. It was 'God and country' that had gotten me into that nightmare. I had no use for any of it. After my daughter's birth, I was open to new possibilities, including looking at religion in an entirely new way." Jeffrey's experience had restored his sense of the holy. For a long time, he had believed that the spirit of God was blotted out in him. Witnessing a birth rekindled that flame inside his own soul. And if it was in him, it could be throughout the universe as well.

Some parents find, in the birth of their child, the birth of feelings that lead them to explore spirituality further. Said one mother, "My labor was a fairly ordinary one, but suddenly in the middle of it, I was hit by the idea—one that I had obviously known intellectually but avoided emotionally—that for millennia women have been doing this. For most of that time, for many women, giving birth might also mean dying. All of a sudden, I was in this place that was midway between birth and death, on the edge of every boundary. I was freaked. But I also knew nothing would be matter-of-fact for me again. And it was not."

Women and men report that "the heavens opened" when their life as parents began. And that, as they say, is the least of it. "Sure, I fell in love when I first saw each of my children," my friend Judy said. "If you want to call it a moment of revelation, go ahead. But to me it is like falling in love with my husband. The first date was only the beginning. I fall in love with Steve over and over again, as we go through our lives together. I am much more in love now than I was the night we met. It is the same with the children."

That is why the blessing says God *renews* creation daily. Each morning is an opportunity to relive those moments of birth and connection and also the moment at the beginning of time—the one we can only imagine through stories. Each morning our souls are returned to us, our world is recreated for us, we are reunited with our children. Each morning we can celebrate this.

What if it were not so?

One of my favorite stories is about the first man, Adam, on the very first day of his life. Night came, and since this was the first time Adam saw darkness, for all he knew, this was it. The black would envelop him and he would never again see the sun, see the animals he had named, see the woman who had been created as his soul mate. So he sat through the night wondering, fearing. And then, as dawn approached, the process he had watched with such sadness the night before began to reverse itself. The sky grew lighter, the birds sang again. Another day had begun. With relief and gratitude, Adam rejoiced.

Our first child was born at 1:00 A.M. on a Friday in December. At ten later that morning, my husband taught a hundred law students the last session of the semester's course. Years later, I ran into a former student of his who had been in that class. I had always assumed that not having slept in over twenty-four hours, Seth had dragged himself through the period. "I still remember him that morning," the student said. "Someone in the back row scratched his head, and the professor noticed it. I have rarely seen anyone so awake."

One of the great religious traditions of the world is devoted to the teachings of a man named Siddhartha Gautama. Once someone stopped him on the road and asked, "Are you a god?"

He denied it adamantly.

"Well, then, are you a celestial being?"

Again the answer was no.

"Perhaps you are a wizard."

Once again, he disagreed.

"Then what are you?"

The man replied, "I am awake."

The Buddha and those who followed him understood that really to be awake is no small matter.

True, with children around, we see more dawns than we might choose. On the other hand, really to see a dawn is no small matter.

Children as Spiritual Teachers

Cheryl Dimof

*Some writings on parenthood suggest that our children are like little
enlightened beings whom we should try to emulate. I've never been comfortable with this view. Young children are wonderfully immediate,
straightforward, and unselfconscious, but they also lack a real awareness
of others' feelings and desires. But certainly our children can teach us a
tremendous amount. In this essay, Cheryl Dimof describes the remarkable similarities between motherhood and Zen training—right down to
the sobering and powerful little "Zen master."*

~

L IKE MOST MOTHERS, I did not come to this wonderful, crazy
world of motherhood looking for a spiritual path. My reasons
for wanting to become a mother were the usual ones: the joys of
watching children grow, introducing them to the beauty of the
world, teaching and parenting them alongside my husband. Perhaps I romanticized the concept of motherhood; I was definitely
not prepared for the real thing: the sleepless nights, the messes, the
constant repetition, the distractions, and the lack of time to myself.

The big question of my life turned from "What is the meaning of life?" to "How can I get a shower today?" and "How much sleep did you get last night?"

After my second child was born, I left the workplace to be a full-time, at-home mom. I was tired of the frenzied pace and conflicting demands of trying to both parent adequately and work a full week. At first I was ecstatic. Here I was, doing the job I loved best with the people I loved most, my kids. Yet as time went by, a question began to gnaw at me: "Isn't there more to life than this?"

It wasn't just that I missed the more immediate sense of accomplishment that comes from being praised for a job well-done, or that I missed the adult interaction, or the sense of contribution to the family coffers that came with bringing in a paycheck equal to my husband's. Perhaps the somewhat slower-paced (although, I'll admit, very busy) life of an at-home mom *had* given me more time to reflect on the meaning of my life, and had led me to grasp something that would bring an even deeper feeling of purpose.

Over the years, I had been sporadically interested in Buddhist philosophy. I found myself seeking out Zen practice and meditation, wanting a way to calm down" from the stress associated with the full-time parenting of young children. I also wanted to enhance my creativity and effectiveness in my family life, and, possibly to try to re-experience the sense of oneness I had felt at earlier times in my life. I was also attracted to the Zen idea of "just sitting." Mothers rarely get to just sit.

In the face of the demands of parenting, just sitting is not an easy thing to do. There is always something else parents must do. As I sat in meditation, my mind constantly wandered to writing checks, doing dishes, going over the myriad household chores that needed to be done. It was difficult to schedule in meditation around early risings, bedtimes, dance classes, and all the other demands of motherhood. Yet I persisted, continuing to see my meditation practice as somehow separate from my role as a mother.

At some point, I decided to seek out a Zen group to sit with. I thought that meditating with others might reinforce my resolve to continue, and that perhaps I would find a teacher who would encourage my practice. When I put the question of mixing the demands of Zen practice with the demands of parenting to a Zen student, she answered that her teacher had sometimes said "raising a family is like having *sanzen* all day, every day." *Sanzen* is a private interview with a teacher that is designed to help one let go of ego attachments and bring one closer to enlightenment (which, in Buddhist philosophy as I understand it, is being able to truly see our interconnectedness and interdependence with one another as human beings). I imagine that sanzen is not an easy thing to take part in. The student's statement intrigued me; however, I realized that it was probably true. More than anything or anyone else, it has been my children who have led me to question my own nature and who have deepened my appreciation for the mystery of life.

In his book *Wherever You Go There You Are*, Jon Kabat-Zinn compares children to live-in Zen masters, and raising them to having an 18-year meditation retreat. As Zen masters go, my oldest daughter, Jessica, isn't bad. At five years, she has just the right mixture of fierceness and . . . well, we're still working on the compassion, but I know it's there. As I sat at the table one morning, eating breakfast and reading the newspaper, she exclaimed, "Mommy! When you eat, don't read, just eat!" Talk about reminding me to pay attention!

Jessica also asks me the most wonderful *koans*. (In Zen practice, a koan is a story or question that cannot be solved using the rational faculties and is designed to bring one closer to enlightenment.) One day, she was anxious to play with a friend who was going to be home in one hour. Every ten minutes or so, Jessica would ask me how much longer she had to wait. Once, after I answered, she asked, "How do you know?" And when I said, "Because I'm looking at the clock." she asked, "How do you know you're looking at the clock?" Question reality! Other favorites of Zen Master Jessica: "What was here before the universe?" "Mommy, why does my tongue have to live in my mouth?" and "How do you know you're not dreaming right now?"

Children certainly can be our teachers. They often act as mirrors, reflecting both our positive qualities and, frequently, those qualities in ourselves that we do not want to own up to or accept. Looking in the mirror of my daughters, I have seen my own shadow and faced my own dark side more than by other way.

The Japanese Zen master Shunryu Suzuki spoke of "beginner's mind," in which the number of possibilities is unlimited. Children have the ultimate beginner's mind. By the time we are adults, we have so much "knowledge," so many preconceived ideas, that it limits our creativity and the possibilities we are able to visualize. Seeing through our children's eyes can help us re-open to a wider range of possibilities. Sometimes when we're stuck in a negative way of thinking about something, our children can offer more positive ways to view the situation. One day, I saw my husband staring out at the backyard, shaking his head in disgust at the number of dandelions that had invaded it. "I want to spray," I overheard him mutter. My oldest daughter apparently heard this as well. "What's wrong with the dandelions?" Jessica asked. She saw them not as a mess of unsightly weeds, but as a meadow of beautiful yellow wildflowers.

Vietnamese Zen master Thich Nhat Hanh recommends posting a note to ourselves saying, "Are you sure?" reminding us to check the reality of our perceptions. Since I have had children, I no longer seem to need that note—my daughter Jessica asks me this question frequently. Her other questions—about everything from how life began, to the minute details of everyday life—frequently remind me of how much I don't know, how much I have yet to learn. This is a humbling and important lesson, especially for those of us who want our children to look up to us as powerhouses of knowledge. (Jessica seems convinced that I am such a powerhouse—I have frequently heard her state, "Mommies know everything!" Somehow, though, this doesn't stop her from arguing with me about everything.)

An oft-told Zen story recounted in Charlotte Joko Beck's *Nothing Special: Living Zen* goes like this: A student asked a Zen master to write something very wise. The master wrote one word: "Attention." The student, disappointed, asked if that was all he had to say. In response, the master wrote "Attention. Attention." The student again felt disappointed and frustrated, and complained to the master that he had asked for something wise. The master responded by writing, "Attention. Attention. Attention." The student, now quite irritated, asked what attention was supposed to mean. The Zen master replied, "Attention means attention."

Mindfulness is an important part of Zen practice, but this word is just a fancy way of saying "paying attention." If we can slow ourselves down a bit from the hurried rush of western life to go at our children's pace for a while, we might notice things we would otherwise miss. "Look, Mommy!" Jessica will exclaim, "This tulip is so pink!" and "Oh Mommy! I love wormies, they're soooo cute!" I remember how beautiful each flower, each sunset, each bug was to me when I was a child. When I can quiet my mind and look through my daughter's eyes, I am able to recapture some of the beauty and innocence of childhood.

Along with helping us to pay closer attention, raising children forces us to ask questions about what is most important, what is "enough." I was confronted with this when my first child was born and I felt I had to return to work to contribute to the family income. Although I enjoyed some aspects of my work, I missed my daughter terribly and feared that I wouldn't be there as she achieved all the big milestones—first steps, first words—and I wanted to share in all of her new experiences. Eventually I realized that I could concentrate more fully on the parts of my life that are most important by changing my attitude toward what is enough. I don't claim to have perfected the art of downsizing, and I admit that I still like to spend money that I probably should not. But I have realized that I have it within my means to claim the family time I want if I am able to live more simply and learn to be satisfied with what I already have.

The speed at which children grow can remind us of one of the most important ideas in Zen, that of impermanence. The idea of impermanence often seems depressing—I think most of us have trouble letting go—but impermanence can also make things more precious. Knowing things will change and pass out of existence makes us appreciate them right now. Isn't it the continuous dance of birth and death, growth and change that keeps life interesting and meaningful?

Finally, children can teach us direct lessons in nonattachment. Of course, we're all attached to our children—we care about and want what is best for them. Yet we cannot fit our children into a mold, or make them conform to an idea of who we think they should be. Children will be who they are; all we can offer is the right environment for their growth and development, whichever way they unfold.

In searching, grasping for a path to help make my life more meaningful, I tended to separate things into the "spiritual" and the "nonspiritual." The spiritual would include such things as meditation, prayer, attending religious services or ceremonies, and communing with nature. The nonspiritual would include things like housekeeping, preparing meals, and changing diapers. It seemed difficult to infuse everyday, mundane, repetitive chores with any meaning beyond the obvious.

When I first attended a Zen sitting group, I was unfamiliar with some of the sutras, or Buddhist teachings, that were chanted at the beginning of the session. I almost laughed out loud when we got to a part of the sutra that read, "Not knowing how close the truth is, we seek it far away—what a pity! We are like one who in the midst of water cries out desperately in thirst." That sounded like me: searching to attain something that I thought I needed and didn't have, when all the time it was all around me.

I then encountered the idea of making everyday activities into a path of practice. If I can do all the myriad tasks that mothers do—changing diapers, cleaning, doing dishes, cooking, chauffeuring—with my full attention (ha), each can become a meditation in itself.

Zen master Shodo Harada Roshi writes, "In the workshop, in the home, while walking, while traveling, while hiking; in the very midst of these we develop and realize our mind's true peace. Wherever we do this is a *dojo:* a place of practice. Each person's home . . . is also a dojo." That my home could be a dojo was news to me. My home usually seemed more like a maelstrom of chaos and disorder. But then it occurred to me that perhaps I was thinking of it the wrong way. Perhaps learning to maintain some inner calm—learning to remain centered in the midst of all the messy, crazy, chaotic, and wonderful demands of family life—was my lesson to learn.

Now, when I remember, I try to follow Thich Nhat Hanh's advice about showing appreciation and gratitude toward my children, my little Zen masters, by bowing to them in a small Zen-style bow—a *gassho*. I remember a woman from my church doing this a few years ago. I thought it was really great, but my oldest daughter didn't; after I respectfully bowed to her, she requested that I not do it again. But we mothers do have our own special practices and meditations. I have sometimes heard a friend of mine chanting, over and over, "Reward the good, ignore the bad." as if it were her mantra.

Although I am still interested in Zen and in meditation, seeking out these small daily practices has helped me open up a little more to learning lessons from my own little teachers who are with me all the time. Though I still find sitting meditation to be beneficial, right now motherhood is my primary path, my practice.

Responding to "Bad" Behavior

Wendy Mogel

Children misbehave; it seems to be part of their job description. Wendy Mogel, a child psychologist, offers a fresh perspective on bad behavior and on the challenges of disciplining our children. Drawing inspiration from the Jewish tradition, she shows us that behavior problems in our children, among other things, demand that we look freshly at ourselves.

~

AS A CHILD PSYCHOLOGIST, I love to deliver my talk "Parent-Control, Child-Control: Where Do Wise Parents Draw the Line?," a lecture about teaching children discipline and self-control, Jewish style. The turnout is usually high, the seats quickly filling with parents whose faces reflect fatigue, tension, and end-of-the-rope frustration. I always know it's going to be a lively evening.

To break the ice I begin by telling these audiences, "Think of your child's worst trait. The little habit or attitude that really gets on your nerves. Or the medium-sized habit that your child's teacher keeps bringing up at parent conferences. Or the really big one that wakes you up at three in the morning with frightening visions of your little guy all grown up and living alone, plotting a shooting spree at the post office. Nod your head when you've come up with it."

Within five seconds, every head is bobbing.

"Good. Now you're one step ahead of where you were a moment ago, because now you know your child's greatest strength. It's hidden in his worst quality, just waiting to be let out."

I'm speaking, of course, about what's called in Hebrew the *yetzer hara*, the evil impulse that is also the source of all passion and creativity. The yetzer hara is a warehouse for our curiosity, ambition, and potency—it's the yeast in the dough. Jewish wisdom teaches us that our child's unique yetzer hara contains the blueprint for her greatness. Our job as parents is clear-cut, if not simple. We are to identify these traits and remove "stumbling blocks before the blind" so that our children's yetzer hara can be channeled and expressed in a constructive rather than a destructive way.

Certain behaviors almost always fall into the category of unacceptable: if a child is repeatedly setting fires or torturing animals, everyone needs to worry. But many behavior problems fall into a vast gray area in which each set of parents has their own threshold of anger, concern, or alarm. Sleepless seven-year-old Miranda may be welcomed in her parents' bed anytime she has a bad dream, while in a different family a child's nighttime visits are considered intrusive and inappropriate. Will's kindergarten fib, "I didn't break it, it broke itself," may be seen by his parents as an age-appropriate and harmless way of trying to wriggle out of a tight spot, while in another family this "lie" is viewed as a serious ethical breach. In different families the same behavior will be defined as feisty or rude, sensitive or cowardly, endearing or irresponsible. But in all families there are some behaviors that cross the line of acceptability. All parents need to civilize their children.

The rabbis teach that children don't naturally behave in a civilized fashion. The British pediatrician and psychoanalyst D. W. Winnicott concurred. The normal child is not a "good" child, he writes:

> What is the normal child like? Does he just eat and grow and smile sweetly? No, that is not what he is like. A normal child, if he has the confidence of his mother and father, pulls out all the stops. In the course of time he tries out his powers to disrupt, to destroy, to frighten, to wear down, to waste, to wangle and to appropriate. Everything that takes people to the courts (or to the asylums for that matter) has its normal equivalent in infancy and childhood, in the relation of the child to his own home.

Any child, then, spends a good portion of his time being bad. The parents' challenge is to teach their child how to control the energy of his yetzer hara and transform it into greatness. "Helping a child channel his yetzer hara" isn't just a euphemistic term for discipline. It means not only enforcing a set of rules but also accepting your child's temperament, respecting his limitations, and shoring up his strengths.

In order to figure out how to improve your child's behavior and channel his yetzer hara, you first need to answer two questions: Is my child's behavior normal? And what part, if any, of my child's problem behavior is a reaction to my own inappropriate attitudes and expectations?

Normal Badness

When parents come to me with worries about their child, the first thing I evaluate is whether or not the problem falls within the parameters of normal misbehavior or unhappiness. "Normal" covers a very broad spectrum, as I learned many years ago when I was a psychology intern in the Department of Psychiatry at Cedars-Sinai Medical Center in Los Angeles.

One of my responsibilities at the hospital was to administer psychological tests to children who were being evaluated upon intake to our clinic. My first month on the job, I tested a seven-year-old whose mother had brought her in to see if she might be dyslexic. After reviewing the girl's Rorschach test results, I ran to my supervisor's office. I had discovered a life hanging in the balance during the course of a routine exam. Her tests were a greenhorn diagnostician's dream.

"Look!" I said, waving the tests at him. "She saw squashed bats, blood! And these drawings! They look so gloomy. She drew a haunted house. She talked to me about death and God. She says she often feels sad and lonely! Should we hospitalize her right away?"

My supervisor carefully examined the entire test protocol. He asked me some questions about my interview with the child and the family.

"She looks just fine to me," he finally concluded. "Might have a reading problem down the line, but seven is generally too early to diagnose dyslexia. You don't need to do anything right now, but ask her mother to stay in touch with us. And you, read this book."

He handed me a copy of *Your Seven-Year-Old: Life in a Minor Key* by Louise Bates Ames, Carol Chase Haber, and Frances L. Ilg. That was the day I learned that a normal seven-year-old's mind, and spirit, is a place of extremes and dark drama, and that a normal seven-year-old's Rorschach can look a lot like the Rorschach of a clinically depressed, suicidal adult.

Your Seven-Year-Old is one in a series of parenting books based on the remarkable research conducted over the past forty years by Louise Bates Ames and Frances Ilg at the Gesell Institute of Human Development in New Haven. On the bookstore shelf the series look like ordinary parenting books: *Your One-Year-Old, Your Two-Year-Old,* on up through the age of fourteen. But inside you will find sensible and reassuring descriptions of natural phases of children's development, written in a manner that conveys the authors' delight in children and their deep respect for them. Knowing what to expect at each stage is a comfort to parents with a suddenly contrary, crabby six-year-old or a morose, withdrawn seven-year-old. Over the years I have made a practice of recommending these books to parents who come to me for guidance. Occasionally I give sections to children to read as well. The children usually say, "It sounds like the person who wrote this met me already!" The books also give such a broad definition of what's normal that if your child's problems don't fit their descriptions, you might—I said *might*—have some justification for worrying.

After I get a detailed description of a child's problem behavior, I interview the mother and father more closely. I ask them if anyone else in the child's life is troubled by the behavior or attitude in question. Is the child having trouble making friends? Is he losing the friends he's got? Is the teacher complaining? Are both parents troubled by it?

In my experience, fathers tend to minimize their children's problems, saying, "I was the same way when I was his age." Sometimes this long view is right on target, sometimes it leads fathers to overlook real problems. Mothers don't typically underestimate their child's problems but their view can also be skewed: since children often show their worst side to their mothers, the mothers may draw a grimmer picture of their child's character or psychological profile than is accurate. When both parents are worried, there is a greater likelihood that a real problem exists. If parents and teacher are concerned and there is trouble with social relationships and school achievement, I'm generally convinced that we're out of the realm of normal troubles. For those families, counseling is in order. Some of the time, however, the children fall well within the normal range. Then it's time for parents to examine their own expectations, attitudes, and *mishegas*.

THE *MISHEGAS* FACTOR

Mothers and fathers usually influence their children more than any other environmental factor, so it's possible that your child's problems are at least partly a reaction to your own *mishegas*. This wonderful Yiddish word, which means nonclinical "craziness," is a good catch-all for the parental neuroses that can adversely affect children.

What forms of well-intentioned but misguided parenting do I see most often? There are a few common tribes: The "we are all equals" parents frustrated that their children won't willingly cooperate with rational, reasonable rules. The "on the go" parents puzzled by their child's desire to stay at home and veg out. There are the anxious parents who continually warn their children about life's dangers yet are annoyed by their fearfulness; the competitive parents irritated by their child's lack of ambition. There are the suffering families where mother and father live with simmering unspoken resentment yet wonder why their children don't seem happy. Finally, there are the "me, me, me" parents who view their children as a personal achievement but neglect to guide and control them.

The good news is that you can limit the damage you do if you are willing to own up to your *mishegas*. It may be that, like so many people, you got away with your particular brand of craziness until you became a parent. In an adults-only world, your perfectionism, moodiness, laziness, impatience, or desire to be liked might have been tolerated by other adults. You might have become expert at rationalizing these bad traits to yourself and others. With children, rationalizations are pointless. Instead of sympathy, you get instant karma. Are you wimpy? Your children will walk all over you if you don't toughen up. Are you moody? Your kids will be moodier. Are you prideful? Your children will test your humility every time you take them out in public. Your character traits will boomerang back at you when you become a parent, reflected in your children's behavior.

RECOGNIZING YOUR CHILD'S WORST BEHAVIOR AS HER GREATEST STRENGTH

If you've honestly confessed to your own craziness and have decided whether or not your child's "badness" is normal, you are ready to work with her yetzer hara. Deborah, the mother of three girls, gave a parenting class this biographical sketch of her four-year-old daughter, Lucy:

She's unbelievably bossy. We all call her the ballet master. When she's with her younger sister and her sister's friends, she tries to choreograph their every move: "This is a very fancy tea party! You have to sit with your legs crossed and your hands in your lap! No loud voices!" If she sees her older sister watching television, she'll ask her whether she's finished her homework.

Her preschool teacher says that Lucy doesn't paint but prefers to walk around the room reminding the other children to put on their smocks, not to mix colors, and to shake off their brushes so the paint won't get too watery. She is constantly organizing and fixing. Last week we went to the library. Did Lucy want me to read to her? Of course not. Instead she found a cart with a pile of books waiting to be restacked. Lucy set right to work, neatly organizing all the books with the spines facing out.

Clearly, Lucy is no shy and amenable follower. Her authoritative nature and penchant for organizing can be wonderful assets that will serve her well throughout her life, as long as she learns to temper them with good manners. In her mother's tone, however, I sensed a helpless, genteel horror at Lucy's behavior. Lucy's forcefulness was embarrassing to her parents, and the embarrassment was preventing them from seeing the positive aspects of their daughter's personality. I proposed that they try to "reframe" their opinions of Lucy. *Reframe* is a term used by psychotherapists that means to rethink your interpretation of an event, often turning your existing opinion on its head.

"Don't view Lucy's behavior as bossy, view it as demonstrating leadership skills," I suggested. "She isn't nosy, she's extremely observant. The fact that she likes to organize the books in the library is a wholly positive trait—imagine how she could apply these skills to keeping her room clean, not to mention the rest of the house."

Parents tend to want contradictory things from their children—docile, "Gallant"-like manners along with extraordinary feats of intellectual, creative, or physical derring-do. But the extraordinary talents arise from the yetzer hara, the unruly "Goofus" side of your child's personality. It's essential that you learn to see those intense, often irksome traits as the seeds of your child's greatness.

REMOVING STUMBLING BLOCKS BEFORE THE BLIND

If you keep running into trouble with your child at specific times—getting ready for school, mealtime, homework, bedtime—it may be that you are inadvertently placing a stumbling block before him. Look for the pattern in the unacceptable behavior, and think about restructuring the situation rather than repeatedly punishing your child for not behaving the way you want him to.

In general, watch for common "meltdown" situations: shopping for groceries with hungry, tired children on the way home from day care; Star-Spangled Chips Ahoy in the cupboard when you want the children to eat fruit for dessert; Super Soaker birthday parties when you've got a child who gets overexcited by a rowdy crowd; MTV on in the house when you don't want your daughter lobbying for tiny tank tops and platform boots.

Preventive Havoc

All children have a barbarous streak. Even if you remove every stumbling block, it is only fair to let them break free from their constraints now and then. The sage Abayei, orphaned from birth, was raised by a nurse he called Eim (Mother). Said Abayei: "Eim told me, 'To raise a child one needs warm water [for bathing] and oil [for anointing]. When the child is a little bigger, he needs things to break.'" When he became a parent, Abayei bought cheap, chipped plates for his own children to break. This wise father understood that all children need a messy, unstructured, unproductive free-for-all every now and then.

Does your child get enough time to horse around? To make noise? To get into trouble? To break things? Arrange to ignore some benign mayhem: send your kids to the backyard with instructions to play with the hose. Turn your back and let them get as wet and dirty as they want. At the end of the summer, let them pull out the remains of the vegetable garden, clipping and ripping the plants to shreds. Direct them to throw cans into the recycling bin. Don't say a word about the noise. If your city-dwelling children tire of genteel craft projects on a rainy day, let them bake a "cake" or poison potion using any ingredient in the kitchen, or buy a bag of party ice and let them throw it into the bathtub. Or take them to the park to play in the mud. Two five-year-olds up in their room and it's suspiciously quiet? Don't storm in immediately to make sure that they aren't showing each other their genitals or lighting matches. Give them a bit of privacy to be children, even slightly naughty ones. Is your ten-year-old choosing to zone out with CDs and some neighborhood friends on a school night or chatting it up online when she should be studying for the state capitals test? Let it go one time. She won't end up an elementary school dropout or in jail. You are parents, not police or undercover agents. Think of all of this as preventive misbehavior, the small temblor that releases tectonic pressure and forestalls a bigger earthquake.

JEWISH WISDOM ON SKILLFUL DISCIPLINE
AND THE PROPER REBUKE

Sometimes removing all the stumbling blocks, recognizing the direction of your child's yetzer hara, and using all the positive spin in the world isn't effective. Your child still does things you don't want her to. Then it's time to use discipline. As with so many aspects of child-rearing, a little bit of forethought and strategy can make this chore much easier.

In Leviticus 19:17 we read, "Do not hate your kinsman in your heart. Reprove your neighbor, but incur no guilt because of him." What does "incur no guilt" mean? Some biblical commentators say it refers to the guilt you would feel if you unintentionally humiliated the wrongdoer during the rebuke. A proper rebuke by a parent gives children a chance to learn about parental values and standards of behavior. Children also learn that it is possible to express disappointment, frustration, or hurt directly without hostility and without causing shame.

Keep in mind that the difference between rebuke and criticism is your intent. Are you scolding your child because you're tired and frustrated? Does he make a good target for your distress because he is smaller than you are? Take a few seconds to ask yourself these questions before you admonish a child.

Don't expect the rebuke to come easily or feel natural. In the Talmud, Rabbi Tarfon says: "I wonder if there is anyone in this generation capable of accepting reproof." Rabbi Eleazar ben Azariah responds: "I wonder if there is anyone in this generation who knows how to rebuke properly." According to Rashi, the major eleventh-century biblical commentator, the trickiest part is delivering a rebuke that carries some sting without shaming the person being rebuked. Protecting others from shame is a central theme in

Judaism. The rabbis taught that shame causes such great pain that it is akin to murder. If we cause someone to redden with embarrassment, it is as though we have drawn blood.

There are three types of sin in Judaism. The first is the *cheit,* or inadvertent sin. The word *cheit* is also a term used in archery to refer to missing the mark or aiming off course. These are sins we do by accident. The second is the *avon,* or sin committed out of the pull of desire. Although we know it is wrong, we cannot resist. The third is the *pesha,* the rebellious sin, done with the clear intention of demonstrating to God (or a parent) that he is not our master. The type of rebuke you choose should fit the nature of your child's transgression.

For the *cheit,* you can point out the error in your child's judgment and let the experience be her teacher. Psychologist Miriam Adahan calls this *rebbe gelt* (rabbi money). Rebbe gelt refers to lost jackets, spilled milk, forgetting a lunch or a homework assignment. The *consequence* of the poor judgment is the "rabbi," or teacher. It's called *gelt* because the lesson learned is worthwhile, as precious as money, and more important than whatever was lost or spilled or forgotten.

How do you rebuke for an *avon?* In the *Mishneh Torah,* Maimonides offers some helpful strategies. If you rebuke or admonish another person, you should:

~ Administer the rebuke in private.
~ Speak to the offender gently and tenderly. (In Ecclesiastes, too, we are taught about the importance of speaking in a soft voice: "The words of the wise man are heard in gentleness.")
~ Remember that you are speaking for the wrongdoer's

benefit and not out of a desire to humiliate or seek revenge against him.

～ Put the rebuke in the context of your high regard for the person being rebuked.

If your child's unacceptable behavior was intentional, if it was not a crime of passion but seems to be a *pesha*—a crime of rebellion or a testing of parental authority—punishment is necessary and justified. Just as you want to avoid shaming a child when you rebuke her, you must make sure not to terrify or abuse her when meting out punishment. At the same time, she needs to feel the sting of her misdeeds.

Judaism holds that children should only be punished if they have been forewarned and know what to expect if they misbehave. The sages teach that God never punishes without previous warning, and as parents we are supposed to emulate God's ways.

A Lifelong Quest for Character

Sampson Raphael Hirsch, the nineteenth-century rabbi and author, had this to say to a mother who complained that her son did not listen to her: "For ten years you did what he wanted, now you expect him to do what you want?" Clearly, we have to get into the habit of disciplining children when they are young if we want them to behave properly when they reach adolescence. Jewish wisdom emphasizes the importance of preparation. You can plan for a wholesome and safe adolescence by getting your child accustomed to discipline from his or her earliest years.

Psychologist Miriam Adahan has a simple formula for effective parenting: one-third love, one-third law, and one-third sitting on your hands. The one-third love we intuitively understand. One-third sitting on your hands means that you'll turn a blind eye to lots of minor transgressions, pick your targets well, and be judicious with discipline. One-third law means that you'll be really tough and unyielding one-third of the time, perhaps much tougher than feels comfortable. The Talmud offers similar advice: when dealing with a child, "be it ever your way to thrust him off with the left hand and draw him to you with the right hand."

This push and pull is emotionally wrenching for parents. To succeed at it, we need to discipline ourselves in ways we may not have done before. This is part of the plan. Judaism teaches us that working on developing *middot* (good character traits) is a lifelong process. Raising children will help you build middot, because changing their bad behavior will probably require you to change yourself. Some of the least glamorous yet most valuable character traits, such as patience, tenacity, foresight, courage, self-control, and acceptance are won in the trenches of parenthood. As you teach your children how to control and direct their yetzer hara, you will discover strengths you never knew you had.

Parenting with Mindful Awareness

Myla and Jon Kabat-Zinn

If we allow it to, parenting can become a path of inner growth and discovery. The Kabat-Zinns liken parenting to an eighteen-year meditation retreat that challenges us to look deeply at ourselves and at human experience. In this excerpt, they emphasize how cultivating mindfulness—a nonjudgmental, moment-to-moment awareness—can be an invaluable resource for parents.

~

*P*ARENTING IS ONE OF THE most challenging, demanding, and stressful jobs on the planet. It is also one of the most important, for how it is done influences in great measure the heart and soul and consciousness of the next generation, their experience of meaning and connection, their repertoire of life skills, and their deepest feelings about themselves and their possible place in a rapidly changing world. Yet those of us who become parents do so virtually without preparation or training, with little or no guidance or support, and in a world that values producing far more than nurturing, doing far more than being.

The best manuals on parenting can sometimes serve as useful references, giving us new ways of seeing situations, and reassuring us, especially in the early years of parenting, or when we are dealing with special problems, that there are various ways to handle things and that we are not alone.

But what these books often do not address is the inner experience of parenting. What do we do with our own mind, for instance? How do we avoid getting swallowed up and overwhelmed by our doubts, our insecurities, by the real problems we face in our lives, by the times when we feel inwardly in conflict, and the times when we are in conflict with others, including our children? Nor do they indicate how we might develop greater sensitivity and appreciation for our children's inner experience.

To parent consciously requires that we engage in an inner work on ourselves as well as in the outer work of nurturing and caring for our children. The "how-to" advice that we can draw upon from books to help us with the outer work has to be complemented by an inner authority that we can only cultivate within ourselves through our own experience. Such inner authority only develops when we realize that, in spite of all of the things that happen to us that are outside of our control, through our choices in response to such events and through what we initiate ourselves, we are still, in large measure, "authoring" our own lives. In the process, we find our own ways to be in this world, drawing on what is deepest and best and most creative in us. Realizing this, we may come to see the importance for our children and for ourselves of taking responsibility for the ways in which we live our lives and for the consequences of the choices we make.

Inner authority and authenticity can be developed to an extraordinary degree if we do that inner work. Our authenticity and our wisdom grow when we purposely bring awareness to our own experience as it unfolds. Over time, we can learn to see more deeply into who our children are and what they need, and take the initiative in finding appropriate ways to nourish them and further their growth and development. We can also learn to interpret their many different, sometimes puzzling signals and to trust our ability to find a way to respond appropriately. Continual attention, examination, and thoughtfulness are essential even to know what we are facing as parents, much less how we might act effectively to help our children to grow in healthy ways.

Parenting is above all uniquely personal. Ultimately, it has to come from deep inside ourselves. Someone else's way of doing things will never do. We each have to find a way that is our own, learning from all useful sources along the way. We have to learn to trust our own instincts and to nourish and refine them.

But in parenting, even what we thought and did yesterday that "worked out well" then, is not necessarily going to help today. We have to stay very much in the present moment to sense what might be required. And when our own inner resources are depleted, we have to have effective and healthy ways to replenish them, to restore ourselves, without it being at the expense of our children.

Becoming a parent may happen on purpose or by accident, but however it comes about, parenting itself is a calling. It calls us to recreate our world every day, to meet it freshly in every moment. Such a calling is in actuality nothing less than a rigorous spiritual discipline—a quest to realize our truest, deepest nature as a human being. The very fact that we are a parent is continually asking us to find and express what is most nourishing, most loving, most wise and caring in ourselves, to be, as much as we can, our best selves.

As with any spiritual discipline, the call to parent mindfully is filled with enormous promise and potential. At the same time, it also challenges us to do the inner work on ourselves to be fully adequate to the task, so that we can be fully engaged in this hero's journey, this quest of a lifetime that is a human life lived.

People who choose to become parents take on this hardest of jobs for no salary, often unexpectedly, at a relatively young and inexperienced age, and often under conditions of economic strain and insecurity. Typically, the journey of parenting is embarked upon without a clear strategy or overarching view of the terrain, in much the same intuitive and optimistic way we approach many other aspects of life. We learn on the job, as we go. There is, in fact, no other way.

But to begin with, we may have no sense of how much parenting augurs a totally new set of demands and changes in our lives, requiring us to give up so much that is familiar and to take on so much that is unfamiliar. Perhaps this is just as well, since ultimately each child is unique and each situation different. We have to rely on our hearts, our deepest human instincts, and the things we carry from our own childhood, both positive and negative, to encounter the unknown territory of having and raising children.

And just as in life itself, when faced with a range of family, social, and cultural pressures to conform to frequently unstated and unconscious norms, and with all the inherent stresses of caring for children, as parents we often find ourselves, in spite of all our best intentions and our deep love for our children, running more or less on automatic pilot. To the extent that we are chronically preoccupied and invariably pressed for time, we may be out of touch with the richness, what Thoreau called the "bloom," of the present moment. This moment may seem far too ordinary, routine, and fleeting to single out for attention. Living like this, it is easy to fall into a dreamy kind of automaticity as far as our parenting is concerned, believing that whatever we do will be okay as long as the basic love for our children and desire for their well-being is there. We can rationalize such a view by telling ourselves that children are resilient creatures and that the little things that happen to them are just that, little things that may have no effect on them at all. Children can take a lot, we tell ourselves.

But, as I (jkz) am reminded time and again when people recount their stories in the Stress Reduction Clinic and in mindfulness workshops and retreats around the country, for many people, childhood was a time of either frank or subtle betrayals, of one or both parents out of control to one degree or another, often raining down various combinations of unpredictable terror, violence, scorn, and meanness on their own children out of their own addictions, deep unhappiness, or ignorance. Sometimes, in the deepest of ironies, accompanying such terrible betrayals come protestations of parental love, making the situation even crazier and harder for the children to fathom. For others, there is the present pain of having been invisible, unknown, neglected, and unappreciated as children.

We believe that parents can best meet their needs by cultivating a certain kind of awareness. This awareness, known as *mindfulness,* can lead to deeper insight into and understanding of our children and ourselves. Mindfulness has the potential to penetrate past surface appearances and behaviors and allow us to see our children more clearly as they truly are, to look both inwardly and outwardly, and to act with some degree of wisdom and compassion on the basis of what we see. Parenting mindfully can be healing and transformative—for both children and parents.

From the perspective of mindfulness, parenting can be viewed as a kind of extended and, at times, arduous meditation retreat spanning a large part of our lives. And our children, from infancy to adulthood and beyond, can be seen as perpetually challenging live-in teachers, who provide us with ceaseless opportunities to do the inner work of understanding who we are and who they are, so that we can best stay in touch with what is truly important and give them what they most need in order to grow and flourish. In the process, we may find that this ongoing moment-to-moment awareness can liberate us from some of our most confining habits of perception and relating, the straitjackets and prisons of the mind that have been passed down to us or that we have somehow constructed for ourselves. Through their very being, often without any words or discussion, our children can inspire us to do this inner work.

Being a parent is particularly intense and demanding in part because our children can ask things of us no one else could or would, in ways that no one else could or would. They see us up close as no one else does, and constantly hold mirrors up for us to look into. In doing so, they give us over and over again the chance to see ourselves in new ways, and to work at consciously asking what we can learn from any and every situation that comes up with them. We can then make choices out of this awareness that will nurture both our children's inner growth and our own at one and the same time. Our interconnectedness and our interdependence enable us to learn and grow together.

To bring mindfulness into our parenting, it is helpful to know something about what mindfulness is. Mindfulness means moment-to-moment, non-judgmental awareness. It is cultivated by refining our capacity to pay attention, intentionally, in the present moment, and then sustaining that attention over time as best we can. In the process, we become more in touch with our life as it is unfolding.

Ordinarily, we live much of the time in an automatic pilot mode, paying attention only selectively and haphazardly, taking many important things completely for granted or not noticing them at all, and judging everything we do experience by forming rapid and often unexamined opinions based on what we like or dislike, what we want or don't want. Mindfulness brings to parenting a powerful method and framework for paying attention to whatever we are doing in each moment, and seeing past the veil of our automatic thoughts and feelings to a deeper actuality.

Mindfulness lies at the heart of Buddhist meditation, which itself is all about cultivating attention. The practice of mindfulness has been kept alive and developed within various meditative traditions across Asia for over twenty-five hundred years. Now it is making its way into the mainstream of Western society in many different contexts, including medicine, health care, education, and social programs.

Mindfulness is a meditative discipline. There are many different meditative disciplines. We might think of them all as various doors into the same room. Each doorway gives a unique and different view into the room; once inside, however, it is the same room, whichever door we come through. Meditation, whatever the method or tradition, is the tapping into the order and stillness embedded in and behind all activity, however chaotic it may appear, using our faculty of attention. It is not, as is so commonly thought, an inward manipulation—like throwing a switch or merely relaxing—into some "special state" in which everything feels different or better, or in which your mind goes "blank," or you suppress your thoughts. It is a systematic and sustained observing of the whole field of our experience, or of some specific element of it.

While it received its most elaborate articulation in the Buddhist tradition, mindfulness is an important part of all cultures and is truly universal, since it is simply about cultivating the capacity we all have as human beings for awareness, clarity, and compassion. There are many different ways to do this work of cultivation. There is no one right way, just as there is no one right way to parent.

Mindful parenting involves keeping in mind what is truly important as we go about the activities of daily living with our children. Much of the time, we may find we need to remind ourselves of what that is, or even admit that we may have no idea at the moment, for the thread of meaning and direction in our lives is easily lost. But even in our most trying, sometimes horrible moments as parents, we can deliberately step back and begin afresh, asking ourselves as if for the first time, and with fresh eyes, "What is truly important here?"

In fact, mindful parenting means seeing if we can *remember* to bring this kind of attention and openness and wisdom to all our moments with our children. It is a true *practice,* its own inner discipline, its own form of meditation. And it carries with it profound benefits for both children and parents, to be discovered in the practice itself.

For us to learn from our children requires that we pay attention, and learn to be still inwardly within ourselves. In stillness, we are better able to see past the endemic turmoil, cloudiness, and reactivity of our own minds, in which we are so frequently caught up, and in this way cultivate greater clarity, calmness, and insight, which we can bring directly to our parenting.

Like everybody else, parents have their own needs and desires and lives, just as children do. Yet, too often, in both big and little ways, the needs of the parent in any given moment may be very different from those of the child. These needs, all valid and important, are simply different, and are often in conflict. The clash of needs in any given moment may result in a struggle of wills over who is going to get "their way," especially if we, the parent, are feeling stressed, overburdened, and exhausted.

Rather than pitting our needs against those of our children, parenting mindfully involves cultivating an awareness, right in such moments, of how our needs are *interdependent*. Our lives are undeniably deeply connected. Our children's well-being affects ours, and ours affects theirs. If they are not doing well, we suffer, and if we are not doing well, they suffer.

This means that we have to continually work to be aware of our children's needs as well as our own, emotional as well as physical, and, depending on their ages, to work at negotiations and compromises, with them and within ourselves, so that everybody gets something of what they most need. Just bringing this kind of sensitivity to our parenting will enhance our sense of connectedness with our children. Through the quality of our presence, our commitment to them is felt, even in difficult times. And we may find that our choices in moments of conflicting and competing needs will come more out of this heartfelt connection, and as a result will have greater kindness and wisdom in them.

Recognizing Our Hidden Wounds

Harville Hendrix and Helen LaKelly Hunt

Many of us go into parenting full of certainty about how we're going to do it right—and be much better at it than our own parents. A few years into it, many of us are surprised to discover new respect and admiration for our parents and, at the same time, are horrified to hear ourselves say the same things to our kids that were so irritating or hurtful to us. "Because I said so, that's why!" In this selection, Hendrix and Hunt, husband-and-wife psychotherapists, explore how our childhoods often come back to haunt us when we become parents—and discuss the importance of identifying when and how we slip into the past.

~

I HAVE BEEN PRIVILEGED over the course of my career as a psychotherapist and teacher to sit with people while they explored their most important personal relationships. For years my practice focused on marriage and how people could build an enduring relationship of love and companionship based on the first spark of romantic attraction. This was a question that interested me, personally as well as professionally, and I devoted several years to developing a framework for helping marriage partners become passionate friends.

When I felt that I had learned enough to be helpful in print, I wrote *Getting the Love You Want: A Guide for Couples.* I did this with the support and inspiration of my wife, Helen Hunt. Since then Helen and I have begun to work and write together. We are now turning our attention as writers to the most challenging and important relationship of all: parenting.

As we became more and more interested in the relationship between parents and children, we came to a conclusion that amazed us: the people who were most successful in marriage relationships were the same ones who were most successful in parenting relationships. Why? Partly because marriage and parenting have some important things in common. For one thing, they share a fundamental progression through stages. Both begin with romantic attachment, move into the power struggle, and then (if you're smart and lucky!) on into healthy interdependence. And we have found that the *imago,* our term for the internalized image of one's parents, shapes both relationships in fundamentally important ways. Our choice of marriage partners is affected by the unconscious internal picture we carry around inside ourselves of our own parents. And the way we parent our children is also powerfully influenced by the internalized experiences we had with our parents during childhood.

At the same time, there are obvious differences between marriage and parenting. You never expect your children to meet your needs in the same way that you hope your life partner will. And your obligations and responsibilities to your children are significantly different from your obligations and responsibilities to your mate.

But at the center of both relationships, if they are successful, is the commitment to become more *aware*—of yourself, the other person, and the ways in which your imago influences your choices and behavior. The people who did well at both marriage and parenting made a commitment to become conscious about the process. They were willing to see what was hidden in themselves and, without prejudice, to understand the connection between past wounding and present functioning.

THE UNCONSCIOUS PARENT

Our use of the term "unconscious" may sound negative, but we don't mean it to be. We contrast "unconscious" with "conscious," and it sounds as though we may be opposing "bad" with "good." But our intention is to use the term "unconscious" as a description rather than a judgment. The term refers to the beliefs we hold, the actions we take, and the behaviors and feelings we experience that are "out of awareness" and therefore out of our control. So universal is unconsciousness and so common are the difficulties that arise from it that we might as well call human parenting unconscious parenting.

Unconsciousness and consciousness occur along a continuum for all of us. None of us are openly aware all the time, or closed and unaware all the time. Our intention here is to help people move to a place where they act and speak with greater conscious awareness most of the time. It is important for us to underscore that unconscious parents are not bad people. They are wounded people who have not had a chance to heal into greater self-awareness and self-acceptance. We are talking, in other words, about most of us.

In fact, many unconscious parents also have wonderful qualities. They are good people who are kind, caring, and committed.

Our purpose is to see the unconsciousness in ourselves and in everyone around us with a compassionate heart. A colleague of ours talks about his experience in understanding how these two seemingly opposed realities can occur in one person. "When I start feeling judgmental, I always think of my grandmother. She is a saint and has been the true mother of our family. There isn't anything she wouldn't do for us. But . . . she doesn't listen. She asks me something about myself and then is silent, waiting for me to stop talking. Then she says something to either approve or disapprove, or says something about herself. She is the center of her universe. I love her, everyone does, and she would do anything for anyone as long as she thought it was what they needed. But she has yet to know the inner world of anyone around her."

LISTENING FOR REACTIONS

Let's start by learning more about what unconscious parenting is. Perhaps we can get a better sense of what the concept means by familiarizing ourselves with how it *sounds*. The following are verbal reactions to the upsetting things kids do or want to do and are examples of what unconscious parenting sounds like:

- ~ *"Don't do that. I told you not to tip your chair back. You never listen. See what happens!"* This from a mother whose six-year-old daughter has just leaned her chair back and tipped it over, hurting herself in the process.
- ~ *"Get out of the street. If I ever see you do that again, that bicycle is gone. Now, put it away. You obviously don't know what you are doing. You are so careless."* This from a father

whose son was just learning to ride a bicycle and who had lost control and ridden into the street.

~ *"You can't be tired. You must just be hungry. Here, eat this apple."* This from a mother whose preschooler wanted to rest at the shopping mall.

~ *"No way are you staying out until midnight. You know what happens. Girls get pregnant."* This from a father whose fifteen-year-old daughter was going on her first date.

These are simple examples of understandable but potentially wounding parental reactions to everyday events. They may be hurtful, but whether or not they are really damaging depends on whether they are part of an overall pattern that violates the essential self of the child. When we refer to unconscious parenting, we mean more than a single overreaction. In its mild form unconscious parenting is everyday experience in which we think we know what our children want or feel, or what they should want or feel. In its extreme form, unconscious parenting is a pervasive pattern of cruelty and neglect that permeates every aspect of a person's life.

LISTENING FOR LIFE STORIES

Unconscious parenting may be the defining pattern of interaction in the family. This example comes from a twenty-nine-year-old woman executive of a national hotel chain, whom we'll call Susan. She sought help regarding her boyfriend's distress about her "unapproachable and emotionally cold nature." She came to therapy carefully groomed and well dressed and had a decidedly successful presence. During the second session the therapist felt that a bond of trust was beginning to build and asked her to talk about herself as a child:

> Susan: You're the only other person I've ever told this to besides my boyfriend. My father killed himself when I was ten, hung himself. I wasn't home when it happened, and I never saw the body. For the longest time, I didn't believe he was dead. I thought maybe he just decided to walk out on us. He was a handyman, and I remember that he and my mother used to argue about some woman who always needed help with painting or the tile on her floor or some repair. But the worst was the dinner table. There were six of us: my mom, my two sisters, my brother, me, and him. I always had to sit beside him on his right. He wanted me near him so he could pick on me. I was the oldest. He never actually hit me. But he would slam down his hand near my plate or sweep my dinner onto the floor or yell at me for no reason. There were about three years there when this happened every night. "What are you lookin' at? You got a problem? Damn right you got a problem. You gonna have one you don't quit lookin' like that." It got so I couldn't eat. Neither could anyone else. I don't know why he picked me out from the rest.

When Susan was asked what effect her father had had on her life, she said she didn't think she carried too many scars. Her denial is not uncommon, because pain of this kind is often repressed. And after she talked for a while, she did concede that she is a perfectionist in her professional and personal life and that she has trouble with the closeness of an intimate relationship. We feel her pain, and the fact that she cannot shows how deeply and completely she has defended herself against her terrible wounding.

REMEMBERING

But unconscious parenting doesn't have to involve neglect, abuse, or abandonment, though it's easier to see it in a story like Susan's. It can be a lot less terrifying and still have a profound effect on the developing child. Here is a story from Harville's childhood that illustrates another way that automatic, unexamined reactions on the part of a parent (or in this case, a surrogate parent) can assume great significance for a child.

When I was about seven years old, I recall coming into the house one day singing loudly. I washed my hands and went to the dinner table to eat, still singing my song. I stopped long enough to join in a prayer of thanks with my sister and brother-in-law, who were in reality my "parents," since my mother and father had died when I was younger. As soon as the food was served, I started up my song again. Suddenly my brother-in-law looked at me sternly and said, "No singing at the dinner table. It's bad." "Why?" I asked. He lost his temper and said, "Just stop or leave the table!" I was stung.

Later, when I visited my brother-in-law as an adult, I asked him about it. He couldn't remember the incident, but he did say that his own mother had told him the same thing. He assumed that singing was "disrespectful to her and sinful." He was taught to eat in quiet reverence, fearing God and the disapproval of his parents.

When I became a parent, I was blessed with children who could sing and loved to sing, and I've always encouraged them to sing anytime, anywhere. But it took years of personal work and a change in my theology to undermine the power of that instruction. Sometimes I still have an uneasy feeling, especially when I join my children's singing at dinner. I hear inside my own head, "Don't sing at the table."

THE COMMON THREADS

What do these examples of unconscious parenting have in common? In each of them, the parent has no awareness of the consequences of his actions and makes no reference to the feelings of the child while he is taking action. The parent acts from his perception of what the child is doing but with *no understanding of how the child feels* or why he is doing what he is doing. The parent is not being consciously intentional, even when he is well-intentioned.

What else characterizes unconscious parenting?

It cuts. First, whether we are talking about a one-liner a parent delivers in a moment of fear for the child's safety or a pervasive pattern of abuse that ignores the essence of the child, *unconscious parenting is a knife.* It slices through the connection the parent has with her child, severing the invisible bond between them. It slices through the connection the child has with the universe, severing the cosmic bond. And it slices into the child himself, severing the bond he has with parts of himself that he now learns are not acceptable and must die.

It is an inheritance. And this brings us to the second character-istic that all forms of unconscious parenting share. *Unconscious par-enting is an inheritance.* Its roots reach back to parenting in ancient civilizations; its branches include parenting in all modern cultures.[1] All unconscious parents in all ages have parented from the deepest center of their wounded selves, perpetuating the pain of their past and repeating it in the future. It is the incomplete, unacknowl-edged, fearful, and shamed part of the parent that speaks and passes the legacy on to his children.

It is unaware. Parents who feel cheated don't realize what they are doing to their children. This is the third characteristic that de-fines unconscious parenting. *It is unconscious.* Freud has given us the language we need to talk about why so much of who we are is hidden from our awareness. And only a small part of our conscious mind is available to us at any moment. It's easy to see why this has to be the case. What if we had to be consciously aware of all the rules of grammar, vocabulary, and syntax in order to speak intellig-ible sentences? What if we had to be aware of how to move our muscles in order to walk? What if we had to be aware of the me-chanics of driving every time we turned on the ignition?

In the same way, the complexities and nuances of our ordinary, everyday mental and emotional experience is available to us a little out of our conscious awareness. It's there. We rely on the accumu-lated wisdom of our past experiences to shape the present moment for us. But we cannot be aware of all of our entire experiential leg-acy at any one time. If we were, we would be crushed by the weight of our own experience.

The wisdom of our unconscious also helps us to know what to do to survive. It alerts us to danger and helps us move fast to coun-teract whatever is threatening us. Without it we might not live very long, because we would have to remember and process more information than is possible in a few critical moments. But as we will see, this survival function is a double-edged sword. Without mitigating counsel from the rational part of our brain, the unconscious can give us bad information—sometimes incomplete, sometimes inappropriate, and sometimes inaccurate. Something can *seem* threatening, and cause us to attack or react as if our lives were in danger, when the appearance is in fact deceptive. In this case we are not under threat and to react as though we were is counterproductive.

The aim here is for selective consciousness. We don't want to be swamped by our perceptions, but it is possible and desirable to open ourselves to more of what and who we are. When we stop denying parts of ourselves and protecting and hiding ourselves from ourselves, we come to know who we really are and accept ourselves. That means that more of our real self is available in our relationship with our children. We no longer need to parent them from a constricted, judged self but can respond to them from an open, accepting, loving self that is freer to accept and love them. It is possible to recognize our unconscious self and, in so doing, meet our own pain. When we meet our pain, we can begin to love our hurt parts back to health.

It causes exaggerated reactions. This brings us to our fourth characteristic of unconscious parenting. *Unconscious parenting is reactive.*[2] Parents know they have touched a sore spot in themselves when they find themselves over- or underreacting to something their child says or does. The hot buttons children push or the words they say that make parents pull back into their own safe space— these say more about *the parent* than they do about the child. Emotionally intense reactions that occur repeatedly and seem excessive to the parent, the child, or another adult are indications of a potential growth point for the parent. She has just identified an issue or a pattern that touches something important and painful in her own life. This is a gift. Parents need to know what their growth points are in order to move beyond them.

It is ignorance. Finally, unconscious parents don't realize that they are often overreacting to their child's normal behavior. This is because *unconscious parenting is ignorant of the specific needs of the child at each developmental stage.* There is no doubt that a child's perfectly healthy behavior can sometimes be annoying. If annoying behavior gets misidentified as problematic behavior, the parent's lack of conscious support can freeze the child's development at that stage. In another of parenthood's many ironies, *parents will have the most trouble guiding their children through the stage that they themselves had trouble with when they were children.*

A mother's fear may cause her to impose her worldview onto her child. She will impute her own fears and worries to her child, and will not fully recognize and honor that the inner world of her child is different from her own. If the mother found it difficult to pass through the exploration stage, for example, then she may be afraid when her daughter begins to explore the world.

REVISIONING THE CHILD

Throughout history the child has been many things to the parent: appendage, clone, laborer, surrogate parent, burden.[3] As part of our revisioning of the parenting relationship, we are advocating that parents adopt a new way of seeing a child, not as one of the above, but as *an emissary from the conscious universe and as a teacher.* A child is born from the cosmos itself into wholeness, experiencing fully the reality of her wholeness. She is born with an innate developmental plan for her completion, which is consonant with the processes of the universe and which includes self-expansion, self-completion, self-repair, and self-reflection. She and we also are a point where the universe becomes conscious of itself.[4]

The job of the parent is to maintain connection to the child so that she can maintain her connection to her parent and so that she can maintain her awareness of connection to the cosmos. She will then be able to expand her connection in an ever-widening circle of relationships through all the developmental stages of attachment, exploration, identification, concern, and intimacy. The parent's responsibility is to meet the needs of his child through these developmental stages and to support the expression of her inborn self.

The conscious parent is able to do this, because he has undertaken his own journey toward consciousness. As he progresses, he takes in feedback from himself, from others, and, most important, from his child.

THE CHILD YOU HAVE

Parents can start by making every effort to see the child they have instead of the one they *think* they have. This is easy to say, but as we have seen, it is hard for many parents to do. Walk into any supermarket, and it's likely you'll hear yourself or some other parent say things like the following: From a mother, gesturing to her teenage daughter: "*Why* do you want to go to nursing school? You just *think* you want to go. You won't like it." Or a father to his seven-year-old son: "You don't want to take ballet. You're strong and athletic. Soccer will be better." Or from the exasperated mother of a tired two-year-old: "Don't tell me you're tired! Do what I tell you to do."

In such moments at least, these parents are unable to form an accurate picture of who their children are or to respond to them in a way that respects their individuality. The feeling you get from overhearing these interchanges is that the parent has decided what's best, and it's no use for the child to argue.

A parent who wants to start seeing the child she *has* must look beneath the surface for the patterns that govern their relationship. A child will respond to his parent's actions and words in certain predictable ways. In her role as parent, his mother will interact with her child according to certain patterns that either interfere with or allow her full comprehension of him as a unique and beautiful person. The parent can become aware of her blind spots, which result not from a cognitive inability to see or understand but from unaddressed needs that belong to her. She can learn how her own wounds are diverting her attention from her child.

Even if the parent grew up in a safe, nurturing environment, she still carries invisible wounds. From the very moment she was born, she has been a complex, dependent creature with a never-ending cycle of needs, and her parents, no matter how devoted, responded to her imperfectly. Her wounds may be small and manageable, but they are still there.

Knowing this can help explain the misfires we all experience in parenting our children—our withdrawals and overreactions that seem to come out of nowhere. If our wounding has been minimal, we are puzzled by these blips on the screen; if our wounding has been deeper, we are thrown into confusion by our exaggerated reactions.

Parenting as Healing Relationship

No matter how old your children are now or what wounds you carry from your childhood, the possibility of healing is open to you. As a parent, you can learn to open your mind to what is present around you and let go of your identification with the constrictions and judgments of the past. Your children offer you a chance for self-discovery while you are discovering who they are. Your relationship with them can be a way to pinpoint the divisions, the opinions, the conflicts, you carry within yourself. They can help you discover what lies beneath your fractured perceptions and enjoy the peace and tranquillity of your original nature, the relaxed joyfulness that is yours to reclaim.

Many of us parents are entrenched in our own view of the world. We don't think of our child-rearing problems as harbingers of healing. Often what we see is disrespectful, uncooperative children who make life difficult for us. But our children can be a light for us if we let them. Even when we are in conflict with them—perhaps *especially* then—children can give us information about ourselves that we can't get any other way. We take a step toward conscious parenting when we understand how our painful moments with our children can become a road map for our own healing journey. Follow the map, and we don't have to walk over the same broken ground over and over again. We can find a new path.

NOTES

1. Lloyd deMause, ed., *The History of Childhood,* first softcover edition, Jason Aronson, Inc., Northvale, NJ, 1995, pp. 51–54.
2. Michael Schwartzman and Judith Sachs, *The Anxious Parent,* Simon & Schuster, New York, 1990. This book is an excellent description of parental anxiety, which is the source of reactive parenting.

3. Lloyd deMause, ed., *The History of Childhood,* first softcover edition, Jason Aronson, Inc., Northvale, NJ, 1995. The author provides a comprehensive history of childhood from ancient to modern times, outlining changing views of the child and of parenting. In the first sentence in Chapter 1 he states that the history of childhood is a "nightmare from which we are just awakening," and he goes on to show that the way most children were treated historically would today be considered child abuse. Since the "child is the father of the man," he speculates on the impact of child rearing on the quality of society. He concludes with a description of the improvement of the welfare of children in modern times as a result of changing views of the child.

4. Menas Kafatos and Robert Nadeau, *The Conscious Universe: Part and Whole in Modern Physical Theory,* Springer-Verlag, New York, 1990, pp. 3, 179.

The Sacred Chaos of Parenthood

Carolyn R. Gimian

In this essay, Carolyn Gimian, a long-time student of Buddhism and meditation, writes about the profound connections between our journey as parents and the Buddhist path to enlightenment. In both experiences, she writes, we are called on to confront the reality of suffering, let go of our ideas, and cultivate compassion. In this piece, Gimian offers valuable and down-to-earth wisdom to mothers of any religious background.

~

PARENTING IN THE TWENTY-FIRST CENTURY is a challenge. We no longer can rely on the certainty of tradition, and our sense of family and our roles as mothers and fathers, men and women, are not prescribed as they once were. So how do we do this parenting thing? Do we try to do it the way our mothers and fathers did it? Do we do it according to the books? Do we turn to our friends as models? From my own experience as the mother of just one beautiful daughter, I think that we do it the best we can, and that we draw on all the influences in our lives—some consciously, some unconsciously—as we make this very consuming, precious, irritating, and rewarding journey. In my own life, a connection with the Buddhist teachings and the practice of meditation has been extremely helpful in finding my way as a parent. It has helped me to realize, for one thing, that parenting *is* a practice. It is something one is constantly practicing and learning from.

AN OPEN-ENDED PATH OF DISCOVERY

One influence on how we parent—what kind of a journey we make day to day as parents—is related to the goals we set for our children and to our view of our children, their childhood, and their future as well. For example, if you believe that it is your role to mold your children's character in a particular way or to protect them from certain potential dangers, that will influence how you relate to them on a daily basis. If you want your child to grow up to be a doctor or a teacher, if you want your child to have strong moral values, if you want your child to go to church or learn to swim, if you want to help your child overcome a particular problem—all of these goals will affect how you behave as a parent and will influence many practical decisions you make along the way. Buddhism views life more as a question than an answer, and, therefore, views a child's future more as a question mark rather than a hard and fast goal.

In that way, the Buddhist approach to parenting is one of discovery, which I think is another way of saying that it is a practice. Rather than fitting experiences with our children into a predefined view or set of goals, we could allow experiences to surprise us and allow ourselves to be surprised about who our children actually are. If you acknowledge uncertainty and change as healthy parts of life, then you are also constantly challenged to give up preconceptions about what parenting and having a family are all about. The anxiety about molding your children into successful adults or making them fit in could be replaced by open space—not necessarily complete relaxation, but at least the space to appreciate your children and to allow them to appreciate themselves and experience their lives as something more than just a path to being grown-up. If children can learn to *be* before they learn to be *something* that is powerful training for all of life, and that is the best practice of all.

THE REALITY OF SUFFERING

One of the first discoveries I made as a parent is that it is impossible to prevent your child from suffering. When my daughter, Jenny, was just a few days old, I realized that I would not be able to keep her free from all harm and that, in fact, I would be the cause of some of the suffering in her life. When Jenny was born, I had a number of complications and a very difficult delivery, one that was actually life-threatening. I was given fairly heavy painkillers and some sedation following the delivery. As a result, I was much more sleepy than the average parent, and so was my daughter. Although emotionally my daughter and I bonded very strongly, the nursing didn't go so well. A few days after she was born, Jenny developed a case of thrush, a rash in her mouth that the doctor said indicated "failure to thrive," and was related to her not getting enough nutrition. Nothing hurts a mother more than a phrase like "failure to thrive." I felt as though I was starving my beautiful baby daughter. Just three days old and already she had a *rash*. I felt terrible. But more than feeling guilty or feeling like a bad parent, there was a bigger message: You won't be able to keep her from suffering. Whether it's this or something else, she is going to experience pain.

This fact of life comes up over and over with children, whether as huge life-threatening issues or as smaller issues, problems, and disappointments: Your child is turned down for a role in the school play. She has a terrible case of colic. He flunks math. He has leukemia. She doesn't have any friends. He won't eat anything because he feels fat. Your daughter is an alcoholic. Children are going to have problems, just as we do. How you and your child work with the issues is one thing, but beneath that is something much more basic: the acceptance that this is the human condition and that we can't exempt our children or ourselves from it. This is essentially the message of the first Noble Truth, the first teaching the Buddha gave. This message, that life is suffering, is powerfully conveyed by our experiences as parents. It is also part of our practice as parents: not trying to fix every problem the second it arises, but welcoming the challenges. They are what we have to work with. From this perspective, when we're facing a difficult situation with our children, we can develop a more open attitude, saying to ourselves "If not this, it will be something else. So why not this?"

LETTING GO

Many of us enter into parenting thinking of how nourishing and wonderful family life will be—only to discover that it's often a textbook case of the dysfunctional family. Whether we embrace the chaos and intensity that come with family life or feel trapped by them, they are facts of life, certainly of family life.

The first time you see your child's face, there is, I think, both instant recognition and an instant shock: Who is this? Where did you come from? Hello again. Why, it's you! Meeting your child for the first time gives real meaning to the "miracle of birth." From the moment when you first meet your child—when you realize that you have no idea who this person is or where they came from, but at the same time that you've always known them and always loved them—children are constantly changing, challenging us to let them be who they are.

In the process of being with children and young adults, I am often surprised to discover that they are much stronger, more mature, and more insightful than I give them credit for being. On the one hand, that's a source of pride as a parent. On the other hand, it's disconcerting to discover that your children don't necessarily need you quite as much as you thought they did. Even when they are at their most helpless, as young infants, children are having their own experience of the world, and they are growing and developing strengths on their own. You can't teach a child to turn over, sit up, crawl, or walk. You can't teach them to talk. You might be able to prevent them from doing those things or to support them as they grow and learn, but the achievements are ultimately theirs, not yours. At times, one feels the emptiness of parenting as much as the pride in children's accomplishments.

Throughout the journey of parenthood, we can learn about letting go and transcending selfishness, which in Buddhism is called egolessness. My husband, Jim, and I were students of the Tibetan Buddhist teacher Chögyam Trungpa Rinpoche from 1970 to 1987, when he died. The day after his death, there was a moment when my husband was feeling quite distraught and emotional. At one point, I was holding our daughter, Jenny, and standing next to him. Jim took Jenny in his arms and said, "She's the only person left in our life now who will make us do things we don't want to do." Then he burst into tears. He was paying her a supreme compliment. I think at some point all parents appreciate that positive quality of demand in relating to their children, although a lot of the time we are just irritated and resentful of the responsibilities that children put on us. Yet through all the everyday activities that you engage in with your children, you begin to see how surrendering to ordinary life brings openness and even joy.

A Humbling Improvisation

Parenting is something we have to make up as we go along. We all begin as novices, whether we acknowledge it or not, and parenthood has a way of showing us our limitations and lack of understanding. Sometimes the humiliations we suffer as parents are on a minute, almost inconsequential level, but this is the stuff of parenting. In our family, this is symbolized by the story of Baby Uh-Oh. This was the doll that my daughter saw advertised on television—yes, we did watch TV in our household even though we knew its evils—the doll that she just had to have.

All parents who have *not* bought some really stupid toy for their children should now stop reading.

Yes, Baby Uh-Oh was a real treasure. She was made of extremely hard plastic, which made her impossible to cuddle, and was very heavy and slightly dangerous if you dropped her. When activated with fourteen size D batteries, Baby Uh-Oh would try to crawl across the floor and would then fall over and start crying until you picked her up and set her off crawling again. Thus the "Uh-Oh" when Baby Uh-Oh fell down. She was loud and obnoxious and, within fifteen minutes of being unwrapped, she was no longer desirable to the little girl who had begged to have her.

The next year, in an attempt to fight the commercial mentality, we vowed not to buy any dumb gifts seen on TV, and to purchase many fewer toys. We had creative ideas: we bought our daughter a lovely rattan hamper and filled it with dress-up clothes purchased from the local thrift store. Her commentary at the end of the gift unwrapping was a rather melancholy "Not much of toys." The next year, we went back to toys. More cheerful.

Whatever way you twist and turn, it seems that as a parent you are bound to encounter disappointment, and are bound to disappoint your children as well. Are there right choices to be made? Certainly there are wrong choices, but it's hard to know if there is really a right way. We let our daughter eat chicken nuggets, and now she's a vegetarian and a much more healthy eater than we are. On the other hand, when Jenny was five or six, a family with three children moved in down the street. They were very strict vegetarians who only ate healthy food and no sugar, a regime imposed by the parents. Their three children loved to play at *our* house. The minute they got in the door, they would hit the cupboards in the kitchen looking for cookies, soda pop, and fruit chews. It was really a bit like a swarm of locusts eating every blade of grass in sight. When one of the girls in this family had a birthday party, none of the kids invited to the party would eat the soy hot dogs or the sugarless birthday cake that were served. Did I feel morally superior because I allowed my daughter to eat junk food? Absolutely, but who made the wiser choice? It's very hard to know.

The Crucible of Family Life

Parenting can push us to the edge of relationship, to a place where we are almost out of control at times. From that point of view, all parents can understand child abuse at some level—because as a parent you feel such unreasonable anger and love for your child. A mature person knows how to limit the *expression* of anger or love, but, at the same time, I think that most of us can understand how emotions can get out of control. I remember once, when my daughter was about ten months old, I was home alone with her for several weeks. My husband was away, and I had very little support or contact with anyone. One afternoon while I was changing Jenny's diaper, she became increasingly fussy and, from my point of view, seemed to be complaining. Finally, feeling overwhelmed, tired, and frustrated, I smacked her on the bottom while she was lying on her changing table crying. I remember that we both looked at each other in shock. She had never been hit before, and I'd never hit her. Actually, it seemed to break the tension, and we both were more relaxed after that. But just as I whapped her on the bottom, I felt myself right on the verge with her, and then I backed away. Then, I felt a huge moment of guilt and felt a sense of failure as a parent. Then I just let all that go and went back to changing Jenny's diaper and getting on with the day.

This experience is, in some ways, no different than seeing how your mind works during the practice of meditation. You find that thoughts and emotions come and go, and you see how you give them energy and how you give them status as important thoughts, important emotions. Working with our thinking and emotional process in meditation helps us to accept more of the intensity and chaos of our lives, both external and internal, and to realize that in fact these dramas are taking place in a much bigger space of simplicity. At a certain point, you drop the drama and go back to following your breath, back to the space. That is also possible in life, and it seems to be an important lesson to learn as a parent. Otherwise, if you feel that you have to hold on to the story line or to the emotions, then you always have an axe to grind and you are driving yourself into what my teacher used to call "the high wall of insanity." You have to keep making your point over and over to justify what you are doing or thinking. Just being able to let it go, let things be, is a powerful space to share with your children.

If we say that we want to talk about parenting as a path, then we are really saying that we're going to look at this everyday activity as a form of meditation practice or meditation-in-action. Parenting gives us a wonderful opportunity to appreciate everyday activity as a vehicle to express mindfulness and awareness. In some sense, it provides an opportunity for us to let spirituality—a spirituality based on the everyday and the mundane—invade the inner reaches of our lives. At the same time, although it may be helpful, and indeed liberating in some sense, to view parenting as part of our spiritual practice, hopefully we're not talking about making it into an ego trip, another "Project" with a capital P. When we do that, we expect to be able to *succeed* as parents—or alternatively, we fear we may *fail* as parents, which can be deadly both for us and for our children. In reality, it's not a question of success or failure.

It is painful and mundane stuff, this being a parent. But at the same time, if we view it as practice, then we understand that it's something we do over and over again—not just as mindless repetition of meaningless activity, but over and over again with interest and attention. We can practice parenting in the same way that we sit over and over again on the meditation cushion, and breathe over and over again throughout our lives. And it's something that we never get perfect, because it's *practice*.

Many Buddhists take a vow to help others in the world and, in fact, to help all sentient beings. I think that most of us would like to help others in our lives, but the idea of helping *everyone* is pretty overwhelming. I find that people often make this vow into an abstraction, distancing themselves from the reality of the commitment, since who can imagine taking that goal seriously? In fact, as far as I know, the only way to help people is through immediate, real relationships. You can't actually help people abstractly or diffidently. You have to jump in and communicate in a direct way with others. You have to make mistakes; you have to get your hands dirty. And it would be truly something to celebrate if, in this lifetime, you could stop causing harm to others, let alone help them. From that point of view, the nitty-gritty qualities of family life are not necessarily something we should try to get rid of. The family could be seen to be like a laboratory or an incubator, a somewhat safe and controlled space in which everyone—both children and adults—can work on relationships and communication.

On the other hand, we also have to be a little careful about viewing the family and children as a saving grace, which seems to be happening more often these days. In what seems to be an unpredictable and often frightening world, we may be tempted to take refuge in our children and our families. But isn't our role as parents to introduce our children to a larger world rather than reinforcing their anxiety and fears? So much hatred and violence in the world have been fostered by people clinging to their own families or clans and establishing a barrier between their little group and their neighbors or the rest of the world. While family life may be nurturing and may provide a certain core or ground of strength, it seems important to recognize that there is more to life. Parenting is not just about building or sustaining good relationships within the family. Children eventually leave the nest we provide for them, and part of the path of parenting is dealing with the empty nest. Eventually, whether through death, divorce, or other circumstances, we will be separated from our children and from our partners or spouses in life. So part of the path and the practice of parenting is also discovering and working with aloneness.

ALL SENTIENT BEINGS

According to Buddhist tradition, we have each been reborn numerous times. In fact, Buddhists believe we have been reborn so many times that everyone we meet in this lifetime has, at one time or another, been our mother. Various chants in the Buddhist tradition make reference to "those who have been my mothers, all sentient beings." This reflects the Buddhist view that all beings are ultimately—and intimately—connected. This teaching encourages us to overcome selfishness and extend our love and compassion to everyone we meet.

When you become a mother or a father, one of the things that dawns on you is the feeling that your child is more important than you are. This is not an intellectual discovery, but an emotional realization that I think is fairly common. You would do anything for your child. Certainly you would give your life for theirs, if you could. In this way, as parents we discover the reality of what it means to put someone else and their needs ahead of your own self-interest. Ultimately, a Buddha, a completely awake human being, is one who treats all sentient beings as his or her children and feels that kind of selfless love for everyone. So, I think that we might occasionally chant, "Those who have been my children, all sentient beings," to express our aspiration to help others and to love them.

My father died fairly recently and I have come to the time in my life—as we all do if we live long enough—when both my parents are gone. I feel immense gratitude to my parents, and I realize all the sacrifices they made for me and how hard they had to work just to raise one child. I also feel my daughter reaching the time in her life where she needs to be on her own. Soon she will be gone. Just weeks from now, she starts college more than one thousand miles away. Even if she returns to live at home, she will no longer be a child in the way that I have grown accustomed to her being. Beyond that, I feel my own death more immediately. It is a complex time, a time of joy, seeing a young woman take flight, leaving the nest and ready to soar on her own, but it is also a time of melancholy and open space. My life is changing, again, as is hers, and neither one of us knows quite what lies ahead.

You reach a certain point in your life where you realize that the big plans and dreams you made will not all be fulfilled. You will not be the queen or king of the universe, attain an unsurpassable brilliant enlightenment that will dazzle others, acquire unimaginable wealth, or get whatever it is you want out of life. Even if you attain such goals, you'll still feel empty. You just have a life to live, and you've lived most of it already! At this point, in a more poignant way, you begin to feel that the smallest moments in life, the stuff of ordinary existence, are very precious. In a way, that's all there is. The rest of it is just conjecture. As a parent you are constantly having your face rubbed in the reality of the present moment. It's a great discipline and it's a gift. Let us celebrate those small moments and aspire to share those gifts with our children, all sentient beings.

"Exceptional" Mothering in a "Normal" World

Miriam Greenspan

Miriam Greenspan is a psychologist and mother of two young women, one of whom has multiple disabilities. In this essay, Greenspan writes powerfully and eloquently about the many challenges of raising a disabled child in a world that fears difference and disability. Whether your child has disabilities or not, this is an important essay to read. It offers mothers of "normal" children heightened awareness and empathy, and it expresses universal truths about parenting.

~

*A*S THE MOTHER OF A CHILD with disabilities, I read with particular interest a review of a book by Michael Berube called *Life as We Know It: A Father, a Family, and an Exceptional Child* in *The New York Times Book Review.* The review starts off: "Some things having to do with children the heart can barely stand. When we read or hear stories telling of such things—parental neglect, parental brutality, babies born addicted to cocaine, political torture . . . we can only lower our eyes and wish for life to be otherwise." Before reading this book, the reviewer admits, she would have "slotted Down syndrome into that list of unthinkables."

My daughter Esther does not have Down syndrome, but she is a child who is visibly "different." In the ten years of her life, I have never thought to associate her with political torture or parental brutality. When I look into her loving, sparkling blue eyes, I don't see something "unthinkable." I had Esther, my third child, when I was 39 years old. I intentionally chose not to do a "routine" amniocentesis, though I knew first hand that not all babies are born "normal." My first child, Aaron, had severe medical problems at birth and died at two months. Anna, my second child, was born radiantly healthy. I have the old-fashioned idea that the child that comes to me is the child I am entrusted to love, and I have chosen to leave my fate as a mother in the lap of nature, rather than in the machinery of medical technology. I have no regrets, despite knowing what I know about the sorrows of raising a child with disabilities.

On the other hand, what *my* heart can barely stand is the fact that many people, like this reviewer, find "different" children "unthinkable" and indeed "lower their eyes" at the sight or thought of them—an apt image for the shunning of disabled people and their families. Her words reflect our society's fundamental fear of "difference." Disabilities like Down syndrome are lumped together with political torture and parental brutality presumably because they are all painful and beyond the pale of "normal life." But the fact is that disabilities (and all sorts of other "unthinkables") are very much a part of normal life—a part designated as "abnormal" and thereby ghettoized socially, fiscally, institutionally, and emotionally from the "mainstream." If they are unthinkable it's because we are unwilling or unable to think about them. One result is the isolation and marginalization of families with special needs.

Webster's definition of "margin" includes "the outside limit and adjoining surface of something: edge" as well as "measure or degree of difference." "Marginalization," a word not to be found in my dictionary, has to do with being shunted to the outer edge of the social mainstream because of a perceived measure of "difference" or "deviance" from socially prescribed norms of family life, motherhood, and personhood. At this outer edge, one has the experience of radical isolation but also the possibility of a "different" view of the center, a different view of family life, motherhood, and personhood that is both subversive and liberating.

In my experience, mothers of children with disabilities are marginalized largely through being socially invisible, an invisibility that is both part of and distinct from the social invisibility of people with disabilities themselves. We just don't exist. Where are we? And what are we doing?

A Day in the Life

On the good days I compare my life with Esther to dancing on a high wire without a net. It is an exhilarating adventure. I feel fully alive and invigorated. I am focused in the moment, and the view is great. But there is always that edge: If I miss a step will I end up in the pit down below, bruised and hurting?

Esther is up and chattering on about the day ahead of her long before I can manage a coherent sentence. Her fourteen-year old sister, Anna, a "normal" child, has been independent in the morning for many years, having learned early this part of her adaptation to being Esther's sibling. At age eleven, Esther can on most days route herself to the bathroom directly and take off her own pull-up diaper. After seven years of painstaking and frustrating morning work teaching Esther how to dress herself, she is able to put on her own undershirt, shirt, underpants, pants, and socks—and these garments are mostly faced in the right direction. She sometimes manages her own leg braces, but her shoes require assistance. This year, however, with the addition of a back brace for her scoliosis, her hard-won quasi-independence in dressing herself has been set back. The body brace needs to be centered and carefully put on or it will do her no good. Its purpose is to keep her scoliosis from worsening and to avert a spinal surgery that holds little promise of helping her, because her scoliosis is "functional"—caused by her "chronic hypotonia" or low muscle tone throughout her body, part of a medical and developmental condition without a diagnosis.

Esther is a slow-moving child in a fast-paced world. She must be on her school bus by 7:35 A.M. Even if she were more able-bodied, there is no way she could get ready by herself quickly enough to make the bus unless she got up at the crack of dawn. Having Esther wake up earlier to take the time to be more independent is not a good option because without enough sleep she becomes more vulnerable to illness. Esther gets sick frequently. Last year, she missed more than 65 days of school. What could be a mild cold for most "normal" children turns into a chronic allergic asthmatic cough that can last for as long as two or more weeks. On the days Esther stays home, inhaling albuterol from her nebulizer and becoming more and more listless, my life and her father Roger's, become centered around her health care and the tricky balancing act of not neglecting Anna in the process.

After Esther is dressed, she eats her breakfast, leaving a small hill of crumbs at her feet, because her hand use is also affected by her condition. She ingests a daily medicinal armamentarium of supplements, herbs, and drugs to strengthen her immune system and treat her asthma. Our dining room cabinet, the kind usually resplendent with knickknacks and tableware, contains four shelves dedicated to Esther's health. The asthma medication and equipment shelf is laden with sodium chloride inhalation solution, Vanceril, Proventil, Tilade, inhalers. Chinese herbs, homeopathic remedies, blue-green algae, and digestive enzymes occupy the second shelf. The Western herbal tinctures share a shelf with DMSO, a non-FDA approved drug that is prescribed by a physician who has researched this medication for neurological conditions. The bottom shelf holds miscellaneous necessities—handweights, theraputty, and spongy balls to strengthen Esther's hands, arm slings used for broken bones. Esther slugs down vitamins and blue-green algae, drinks her "power drink" and foul-smelling Chinese brew, and inhales her Vanceril without complaining. She's a pro at pill popping and medications.

After an hour of labor by Roger or an hour and a half by me (Roger is a faster helper than I am), Esther is launched to school. Each morning, as she gets on the bus, I silently pray that she will come back in one piece. By eight years of age, Esther had fractured eight bones. Several of these breaks were from simple falls that most kids would just brush off. She is at risk for these multiple injuries and fractures for reasons that are not well medically understood. *Goddess, I release her into your care, and I pray that you guide and protect her.* My ritual prayer as she gets on the school bus or ventures anywhere out of my sight helps me let go of the hypervigilance that I have had to exercise in being her mother.

It is usually Roger who picks up Esther after school. He has an academic schedule, while I see clients in the afternoon. One of us accompanies her to a variety of afterschool activities that include vision therapy (for her problems with tracking, focusing, and depth perception), Hebrew school, music therapy, and choir.

Fortunately, Esther receives occupational therapy, physical therapy and speech therapy at school, otherwise there would not be enough hours in the day to take her on her daily and weekly rounds of special-needs care. Or alternatively, it would require that one of her parents take a permanent leave of absence from work, a sometimes inviting but highly impractical possibility. Every several weeks, depending on her state of health, she visits one or more of a dozen health care providers or therapists including pediatrician, orthopedist, asthma and allergy specialist, otolaryngologist, acupuncturist, and chiropractor. Visiting doctors is a permanent way of life for the parents of a child with special needs. In Esther's case, so is the continual search for ways to help her with a condition that has no name. Her mild hearing loss, chronic allergies, sinusitus, asthma, lowered immune system, severe difficulties in the perceptual-motor realm, generalized learning disabilities, foot deformities, hypotonia, poor balance and coordination, and vulnerability to bone fractures are all part of a puzzle that no one seems to be able to fit together. Nor do we know if knowing how it all fits together would be particularly helpful to her or to us. In the meantime, we research ways to help her, and my "Esther" files, which fill a two-drawer file cabinet, continue to grow.

In the evening, one of us helps Esther with her homework, which is done on the computer because her handwriting is minimal. Her nightly bedtime routine includes being helped with her bath and evening medications, being read to, and having her back and feet massaged before she goes to sleep. Esther is usually in pain by the end of the day; the muscles of her back, neck, feet, and legs are tired and sore. The massage is also to help her relax because though exhausted, she often has some trouble turning off her energy and becomes maddeningly perseverative when she's tired. The last words that Esther hears each night are my prayers: *May your healing be complete, may you stand on your own two feet. May I be patient with you, may you be patient with me. May you always be full of life and love and know that you are loved. God bless you and be with you. Now go to sleep.*

I have assistance in raising Esther that far surpasses what mothers of children with disabilities received in other eras or receive now in other societies. I am entitled to $900 annually for "respite care" from the state of Massachusetts, to be spent for a "respite care worker" who gets paid $9.00 per hour. Esther's education in an integrated program in a private school is paid for by the Boston Public School system, thanks to the "766" state law by which each child is entitled to an education in the "least restrictive environment." The synagogue to which we belong pays for an aide in Esther's Hebrew and Religious school classrooms. I live in a city that puts out the excellent *Exceptional Parent Magazine,* which brings me monthly installments of relevant news, information, and support.

Most of all, I am not alone in raising Esther. Roger is as much Esther's "mother" as I am. (She inadvertently still uses "Dad" or "Mom" interchangeably to refer to either one of us.) Coparenting of this kind is the exception, not the rule in the care of most children. This is especially so for children with disabilities, whose parents have a significantly higher rate of divorce than the general population and who are then raised by single mothers. Roger's involvement in Esther's care—and the privilege of his academic schedule, which permits him to spend much more time with Esther than most working fathers could—allows us to break down the labor. Roger does more of the morning and evening daily maintenance, while I am Esther's overall care coordinator. On average, I spend as much time taking Esther to doctors; coordinating her care; and researching educational, therapeutic, and medical resources as I do working in my profession as a psychotherapist, having limited my private practice and consulting to part-time since her birth.

Though Esther has two "mothers," it's still a rare day when either one of us feels adequate to the job. There is always something essential that falls to the ground while we juggle the other six balls. On a bad day, I feel like Sisyphus of the Greek myth. Pushing his huge stone up the mountain, he exerts a prodigious effort to get it to the top. And just as he does, the stone begins to roll down the mountain due to the force of gravity, rolling right over Sisyphus on its unrelenting way down. He must then start all over again—only to confront the same crush, endlessly into the future. Just when things seem to even out, a new set of daunting challenges presents itself. There are times when everything seems to fall apart—when Esther's normal daily needs are complicated by prolonged periods of illness and I am confined to my house, my spirits dimmed by the sound of her asthmatic cough; when I must put the rest of my life "on hold" in order to tend to her; when all sense of order disappears under a pile of unfinished tasks. At these times, I enter a state beyond fatigue that is akin to despair.

Furthermore, the traditional social expectations of motherhood die hard. Most mothers internalize a standard of mother care in which the expectation is that the fundamental responsibility for the care of the child is mother's work. Those of us who cannot afford a live-in nanny or full-time aide, or who do not wish to hand to professionals the total care of our children, still have to grapple with this expectation. This feeds a sense that we are responsible for a job that no single person is capable of doing, which is a recipe for feeling inadequate.

The pain and exhaustion of the hard times has as much to do with how our society throws families in general onto their own individualized and atomized resources—resources often scant enough for the "normal" family and inadequate or catastrophic for the "disabled" family—as it does with Esther's needs. It has as much to do with not being able to afford all of the out-of-network, out-of-pocket health care that she could use as it does with her chronic medical problems. It has as much to do with how poorly our society deals with "otherness" as it does with Esther's "difference." If, as the saying goes, "it takes a village to raise a child," then special-needs children need that village even more than others do. The absence of that village—of community support and of an honest, balanced, informed, communal understanding of the joys, challenges, and difficulties of raising a child with disabilities—not only contributes to what's disabling about disability, but is at the core of what perpetuates a sense of mothering at the margins.

The Silence of the Mothers

Many mothers of children with disabilities prefer to keep their pain and exhaustion private, not wanting to fuel the argument that children with disabilities are a "burden" to their parents and to society. This is a self-enforced silencing that is part of what it means to be "marginalized." As I see it, mothers disproportionately shoulder the "burden" precisely because the social marginalization of mothers and of disability are at the heart of what's overwhelming about raising a "different" child.

I recently attended a conference on mothers and daughters at which one of the speakers was a mother of a grown child with multiple physical, cognitive, and developmental disabilities. She spoke about how mothering such a child is in many ways no different than mothering any child. One is called to love and to nurture, to discipline and to guide, to accept and enjoy the child for who she or he is, to lay the fertile ground in which the child's individual gifts can flourish. I was struck by the fact that only in a society in which the intolerance of difference is endemic to our way of thinking is it necessary to make the point that our children, whatever their "special needs," are still children, and that we mothers, whatever our differences from "normal" mothers, are still mothers. Is this "normalization" of difference necessary? Sadly, yes.

I was prompted to add a comment to this speaker's words— that however much we are like "normal" mothers, mothers of children with disabilities also do many things that "normal" mothers don't do and think about many things that "normal" mothers don't think about. Feeding a child through a gastric tube inserted into the stomach; tending to her toileting needs throughout her life; re- searching the medical literature on a particular diagnosis; managing the complex bureaucracies of special education, medical treatment, and insurance companies, to cite just a few examples, are generally not what mothers envision when we sign on for the job. In my experience, it is rare for mothers of children with disabilities to tell it like it is when it comes to how atypical a typical day in the life can be. In response to my comment, the speaker at this conference admitted that for many years she kept silent about the physical and emotional demands of the daily routines of caring for her daughter, believing that she must bear her lot stoically to be a "good mother."

The pressures of what it takes to be a "good mother" are ap- plied to all mothers, but are particularly isolating when the chal- lenges of being a "good mother" are heightened by disability. I have felt this kind of pressure from school officials or doctors when advocating for Esther and know several mothers who have had similar experiences. Anything less than a serene or stoic attitude to the difficulties of raising our children may be counted as a failure of "good mothering." To speak of the burdens along with the pleasures of mothering may be seen as proof that we are "unresolved" about our children's disabilities, too hyperinvolved and unable to "separate" from them adequately, thus damaging their self-esteem or worsening their disabilities. Silence about the difficulties and necessary sacrifices of raising our children seems to be the requisite of "good mothering."

This is one of the main reasons I include my unadorned chronicle of a day in the life. If my day with Esther sounds laborious and difficult, this doesn't mean that mothering Esther is not also a delight and a gift. But neither does the delight cancel out the difficulties. I think it is important for all mothers to resist silencing, censoring, and "disappearing" ourselves for the sake of holding up the cultural image of "good mothering."

INVISIBILITY

When Esther was three years old, we spent a few weeks at a family meditation retreat in Barre, Massachusetts. Esther had learned to walk six months before, a newly born colt. One afternoon I stood with her on the great green lawn, watching as the able-bodied children ran and jumped and tumbled. Someone's daughter, a practiced and near-professional gymnast, was working out on the lawn, doing cartwheels and spins that seemed as effortless as breathing. My awe at the agility of the human body had been heightened by the troubles that Esther has with movement and coordination. I took in this athletic and graceful performance with a mixture of awe and grief, admiration and envy. As I wondered if I would ever be able to look at an able-bodied child again without that particular mix of feelings, the man who stood next to me on the lawn, a practiced meditator in the Vipassana (Insight) meditation tradition, said of the young gymnast spinning a cartwheel before us, "Isn't she just superb? Children are so graceful and agile, aren't they?" I was speechless. I felt in that moment that this man was addressing himself to a ghost, and that I was that ghost, my substantiality not perceivable to him. This young girl was most certainly superb, graceful, and agile. But his use of the universalizing plural noun, the absoluteness of his exclamation that "children are so graceful," addressed to me as my Esther, barely able to stand without falling and as easily blown over as a leaf in the wind, stood in plain sight before us, made it clear that this man, trained in awareness, was simply not *seeing* Esther. She was as invisible to him as I was. He saw only the gymnast and, from this partial sight, spun his tales about children.

The generation of children born to the baby boomers is in fact the most visible generation of children with disabilities in the industrial West. Handicap accessibility has arrived on the scene in the past two decades. We now see people going about their business in wheelchairs in ways that were once impossible. As recently as twenty years ago, mothers of children with Down syndrome or other birth defects were routinely advised on their birthbeds to institutionalize their "defective" offspring. We see "different" children in public in greater numbers than ever before. "Sped" or special education is an expected part of most public school systems. Still, our senses can close themselves off to whatever we do not wish to see. And this closing off on the part of the able-bodied keeps both child and mother on the periphery of consciousness, the outside edge of everything we call "normal" life. We are generally educated in our society to not see the disabled and their families, who appear to be a blot on the very idea of the "normal" family and of "normal" life itself.

Mothering a "Different" Child in a "Normal" World

Crippled. Disabled. Handicapped. Child with disabilities. Special-needs child. Physically challenged. Differently abled. Developmentally delayed. I don't like any of these words. They are either stigmatizing and limiting (crippled, disabled, handicapped), thereby contributing to the person's "disability," or they are patronizingly euphemistic (physically challenged, developmentally delayed), a reaction to the stigmatizing and limiting words. Or they are just "politically correct" but largely useless (differently abled). Our language has no way to express the condition of someone who has physical, mental or educational needs that are more than what is typical of others, without invoking a standard of normalcy or patronizingly avoiding it. It has no way of describing a condition that requires the help of others in a respectful and not paternalistic way.

One day I was rushing the kids to the dinner table and my oldest daughter Anna wasn't sure she wanted to eat with us at that hour. To her question "Why do I have to eat dinner when you do?" my quick and unthoughtful answer was "Because I enjoy eating dinner like a normal family." Without missing a beat, Anna exclaimed, "Mom, there's no such thing as normal!" "You're absolutely right," I said, grateful for how Anna always catches me up in my thoughtless replies. "I want you at dinner," I corrected myself, "because I enjoy your company."

A sign in my private practice psychotherapy office reads "Why be normal?" Growing up, I never much took to the idea of normalcy. As an adolescent, I remember praying, like the girl in the play *The Fantasticks*, "Please, God, don't let me be normal." With a child's-eye view of the world that came from being the daughter of Holocaust survivors, I did not find the measure of the "normal" a comforting one. From an early age, it seemed to me that normal people had committed all the small, daily, ordinary, and extraordinary acts that become, when all was said and done, the Holocaust. And that normal people had let it happen. I didn't want to be that kind of normal.

The problem lies in our culture's entire way of categorizing people into normal and abnormal, mainstream and deviant. We can't even imagine what it would be like to think outside of this dominant dichotomy and its inherent ideology of difference. Who are the normal? And who the different? In our culture, the norm for normal is the white male without any *visible* physical or mental deficits. The "normal" male is the standard-bearer for qualities that are highly valued in the culture, such as independence. But judged against a standard derived from the margin, for instance, a more female norm of human empathy, the "normal" (male) person seems rather deficient. The difference between normal and deviant depends on where you stick the sign that says "normal starts here." Philosophically, morally, and practically, the fundamental idea of "normal" is troublesome, erecting a hierarchy that inherently reproduces a false sense of competence or a debilitating sense of shame in those who fall into the normal or abnormal categories, respectively.

Questions of normalcy and difference are complex and fraught with moral, philosophical, and practical dilemmas and ambiguities.

But the way that they affect me as the mother of a child who is not "normal" is quite simple. The shame of the "not normal" is a condition that one must continually refuse to carry. And refusing to do so makes every day an opportunity for resistance. Accompanying Esther to a new classroom, taking a walk with her in the arboretum, taking her to a play, these everyday occurrences sometimes result in contact with people who blind themselves to Esther's disabilities out of ignorance or fear, or who gape unabashedly at her in a way that they would not do with a "normal" person. Shame easily comes with this territory. Sometimes the staring stems from simple curiosity, which is why I always prefer, as does Esther, to have her special difficulties and needs openly known rather than hidden from others. On the other hand, I have seen children back away from Esther, refuse to sit next to her, stare in a hostile fashion, or shun her as though the shame of her condition might rub off on them. In some instances, Esther is oblivious to this, probably because she doesn't understand social cues as well as she might or because of her perceptual difficulties. The more she becomes aware of her otherness, the more she talks to me about feeling bad. We have talked frequently about how some kids tease or ignore other kids as a way of trying to feel better about themselves, or because they are ignorant. She has heard me say, "No matter what someone may say or do, never forget that no one is better than you." She has also heard me repeat, "You're very good at doing hard things—and that's something many others, to whom things come more easily, are not so good at," and "Whatever you can or can't do, you are a generous, loving, wise person, and nothing is more important than that." In reminding Esther of her worth, I find a way to lift the mantle of shame that can fall so swiftly and silently on the shoulders of one who sees her child treated as "other." The shame of the "not normal" is ultimately the shame that our culture must bear for its intolerance and fear of "difference." I remember a funny song Anna made up years ago, with the refrain "We're all the same in a special way," incorporating the resistance that Anna is learning as Esther's thoughtful older sister. I wish the "normal" world could learn this song's simple truth.

SPIRITUAL RESISTANCE

Mothering Esther is about parenting without a developmental map. This is in some sense true for all mothers because every child is unique, but for me, there are none of the usual reassurances of "normal" one-size-fits-all parenting and one-size-fits-all models of child development. There is a freedom that comes with this kind of marginalization. The questions about Esther's future hang uncertainly in the air: Will she or won't she have the same needs and disabilities tomorrow as she has today? How many of them will impove? How many remain? Will she be able to live independently? With what kind of help? None of us really know how our children will end up, but we may surround ourselves with illusions of safety and certainty. In mothering Esther, not knowing is the name of the game. It teaches the spiritual discipline of living in the present moment while planning for a future that is, by definition, uncertain. There are days when this challenge brings nothing but anxiety. But as a whole, I believe it has been a profound teacher of spiritual steadfastness and courage. It is Esther herself who is my role model here, teaching me to experience my life with her and my family as a challenging adventure.

Our family is vacationing in Vermont. Esther is the first child with disabilities at the Farm and Wilderness Barn Day Camp. She is six years old and determined to ride a bike. Roger and I rig up a souped-up tricycle that we think will be safe for her. We take turns teaching her. Anna, eager for Esther to learn, spends some time teaching her as well. It seems Esther has the essentials down. There is a moment where I take a deep breath and turn indoors to cook dinner.

I let go of my eternal mother's vigilance. For once I treat Esther like a "normal" child, and with just a moment's hesitation I simply leave her on the bike. Roger and Anna are at her side. Two minutes later I hear her wail. I run out just in time to see Esther spill off the bike. She soon stops crying and wants to get back on. I look at her hand and help her on, but then see that she seems to be in mild shock. Is her arm broken?

Later, as we sit and eat dinner, Esther says quietly, "I can't use this hand." An X-ray at the local Vermont hospital confirms the fracture in her wrist. It is the fourth fracture in six years. At the hospital, Esther is her usual brave and friendly self. She is cheering us up. She is complimenting the doctor on what a good job he is doing putting a cast on her arm. Later she asks him if she can swim. When she is told she cannot swim with the cast on—and that means for the rest of the camp season—she pauses for a second, then says, "That's OK, I'll stay down by the waterfront and put my legs in the water, or I'll go up to the barn with the counselors and sing." Esther loves swimming more than anything in the world except for maybe ice cream and pizza. It is one of the only things she can do where she doesn't look weird and her body is relieved of the constant pull of gravity. How can she be so accepting? She only wants to be included, and finding a way to include herself at the camp, even with her broken wrist, she is happy.

The next morning, she eats breakfast with her good arm and

sings a little made-up song that goes, "When you open up your love, love will come to you." She soothes her hand, calling it "beauty star" and sings lullabies to it to make it feel better. Later on, she laughs, "It's just a broken hand. Ha!" Esther teaches me how to mother her. And she is an exceptionally good teacher because just as her muscle tone, her cognition, and her neuromotor system are not "normal," so it is with her ego. She is a little buddha who finds something to be grateful for in the present moment and enjoys it, continually teaching me about love without conditions, care without ownership, the sacred in the broken.

Still, I cannot make her the wisdom child. She has her own struggles and pain. She has no close friends her own age. She is sometimes lonely. She is too attached to TV, her dependable pal. She gets frustrated and perseverates. And I get frustrated, weary, and angry. I pray to be worthy of her. Like dancing on the high wire without a net, I have to let her try, to let her risk, to let her be frustrated and uncomfortable, in order for her to develop new skills. But each time I take a breath and wonder if she'll survive. I know I can't protect her, I can only fight for her and then let her go. I try to remember, where there is fear, there is power. And when I do, I can be a source of healing energy for her and she for me.

Esther herself is the best source of whatever courage and resistance I muster in the challenge of mothering her. She has taught me acceptance and gratitude for each moment in a way that has brought a very special kind of joy into my life. She has helped free me of the shackles of a driven achievement orientation to life that comes from my early family training, and the entire culture's premium on performance and obsession with "success." Esther teaches me the absolute value of life, a value that has nothing to do with what she can give me by way of reflecting back my own ego. I am rarely proud of her in the "normal parent" way in which parents narcissistically take credit for their children's accomplishments. When she sings her heart out at a musical recital, it is not her near-perfect pitch that I take pride in. What I feel is a sense of awe and gratitude for the amazing beauty of her spirit and the way that it comes through her in song, warming the hearts of those who hear. Everything that Esther is, she has made herself—against tremendous odds. It is not "pride" I feel but genuine respect for who she is as a person. The flip side of Esther's special needs are her special gifts: open-hearted generosity of spirit, compassion, emotional wisdom, and joy in the midst of limitation.

When I told a relative some time ago that Esther's disabilities would be ongoing, that she would not grow out of them as we, her doctors, and teachers had once hoped, he referred to Esther as "the worst nightmare a parent can have." I understood this as his way of trying to be empathetic, though he could only imagine a life of "non-normal" parenting as a nightmare, not as a gift. Actually, I could think of many things I would consider parental "nightmares": murdered children, children with AIDS, teens dying in car crashes, adult children who are battered by boyfriends or raped, children who grow up and work for the Pentagon. As she is, without the comparisons to "normal" by which her life appears to some to be a nightmare, Esther is a continual source of delight and spiritual sustenance in my life. I am blessed to be her mother. Given a choice, I would not choose her to be other than she is, though like all mothers who love their children, I would want her to have a life of good health. If there is a nightmare here, it is my fear that the world, when I leave it, will not be sufficient to hold her or to see her truly. The unanswered question is: Will her gifts find their place in a world not yet worthy of her, or of any of our children?

Part Three

~

Why Is Being a Mother So Hard?

Guilt—What It Does to Us

Anne Roiphe

In this selection, Anne Roiphe, noted writer and feminist, cuts to the heart of the matter: the ever-present problem of maternal guilt. What is it? Where does it come from? What is its toll? Many readers will recognize themselves in Roiphe's personal stories. This is painful terrain. She does not propose a solution to the problem of guilt, but Roiphe's honesty seems an important starting point. What if we all became this open, honest, and inquisitive about our maternal pain?

∼

I AM DIVORCED. My first child is two and a half. My mother has died. I have to find a way to make a living. I'm running out of money. I am sitting in the playground watching my daughter climb up and down the jungle gym. She is reckless, bold, careless, and flushed with pleasure. I am tense, frightened, hold myself back from stopping her. I want her to explore. I want her to have dirt on her knees, to dare. I also want her to be careful. I bite my lip till it bleeds. I bring her home and fix supper. She doesn't want what I have prepared. I sit with her and beg. I make faces, I read a story. I put on a record. I give her crayons. I prepare something else. She is pale now and tired. I give her a bath. She moves away from the washcloth. I chase her. I notice a mole on her shoulder. Is it growing? I should ask the doctor about that. I think about melanoma. The doorbell rings. The baby sitter has arrived. I have a graduate school class. My daughter knows this baby sitter. She sees her and climbs out of the tub and grabs my knees. I need to get my books. I need to comb my hair and change my clothes. I carry my daughter in my arms as I do these things. Her fingers are pressed into my neck. I set her down. I am going. I am going out the door. My daughter begins to scream. She screams not like a child in pain but as if a nightmare were progressing, as if deep within her everything was falling apart. These are shrieks and sobs combined. She loses her breath, her face is red. She gasps for air. "I will be back. I always come back. I will be back by eleven o'clock. I promise I will be back," I say. She screams harder, she tries to grab my hair. I know she is screaming because she has only me, I am the sole parent. That is my fault. I pry her loose. I know what I have to do. I open the door. The baby sitter holds my daughter in a firm grip. I run out the door. I ring the elevator bell. I hear her screaming. I hear her as I ride down the elevator, all the way to the first floor I hear her cries. I am soaking wet. I have perspired through my shirt. I feel faint. Should I go back upstairs? I wait a moment or two. My heart stops pounding. I head off toward the subway. The churning in my stomach is not all sympathy and love. Something else, a desire to leave has entered. This only makes me more guilty, guilty as charged, leaving a child. I have never been more miserable.

I understand perfectly what Adrienne Rich meant by "the invisible violence of the institution of motherhood . . . the guilt, the powerless responsibility for human lives, the judgments and condemnations, the fear of her own power, the guilt, the guilt, the guilt."

The child may always wish to be with the mother but the mother often has other desires, friends, work, family. She is attracted, distracted, needful of the outside world just when the child requires her to be focused, steady, home, near. What mother hasn't had secret dreams of escape? What mother hasn't had moments when the strain overwhelms, when the child whines once too often, when the exhaustion of soothing a colicky baby grows too intense, when the struggle between siblings sets off a desire to flee? What mother hasn't wondered sometimes if she really loves her children, enough, too much, at all? What if she really has to go to work?

Adrienne Rich writes most pointedly about this mother guilt: "For years I believed that I should never have been anyone's mother, that because I felt my own needs acutely and often expressed them violently, I was Kali, Medea, the sow that devours her farrow, the unwomanly woman in flight from womanhood, a Nietzschean monster." This is expressed in somewhat hysterical language but the truth in it is recognizable even to those of us with less volatile or literary temperaments. There is inherent in motherhood a continual giving up of self, and few of us take to that without resentment, which itself creates a river of guilt. Adrienne Rich is able to call on the figures of Kali and Medea because culture has provided images of the all-purpose destructive woman, the cruel and consuming mother who like an animal gone wild will eat her young. These are male-created images but women recognize them too. We fear the destructiveness inside ourselves. Most of us are afraid that if we caught our true face in the mirror we might see not the most beautiful queen in the land but the wicked stepmother, the Medusa who turns her enemies to stone. This makes us feel guilty.

One of the reasons it's hard to express satisfaction with your life when you have children is that everywhere, every day there is anger. Not the life-threatening kind that caused Susan Smith to kill her boys, not the dark rage of depression that caused Sylvia Plath to put her head in the oven with her two babies in the house, but the quick summer storm kind of anger, the slow burn anger, the underground anger that sometimes affects what you do or say without your even knowing that it was there. There are the terrible twos when a child asserting independence refuses to wear mittens on a freezing cold day and for a moment your frustration turns you into a wild thing. There's the other kind of anger that comes when you need sleep and the child wakes or you need to soak in the bath and the child wants you to see his block tower. There's the anger that rises out of frustration when a child gives up the violin after you hocked the family jewels to buy him the instrument and pay for the lessons. There's the bleakness that follows a bad report card when you know a child can do better. There's the hard-to-express kind of anger you feel when you know the child can't do better. Anger is everywhere in the rough-and-tumble of child rearing as you find out what you can't tolerate, what kind of a demon witch you really are, what causes you to flare, to stifle fury or to stuff it back down the throat, to let it out all of a sudden: the room is a mess, the dinner not eaten, the fight with a sibling, the toy broken, the rule broken, the thing undone, the thing done. Added to the complication are old angers that belong in scenes long gone, angers against a father who never took you to the circus, the way you took your child who is right now jumping over the seats, or angers against a mother who wouldn't let you have or told you that or died too soon. These old angers get a second chance to do damage when children evoke, provoke, provide opportunity. Mastering anger, not letting it trample the child, not letting it turn inward and strangle the spirit, this is a task that many of us cannot do or do not do as well as we would have liked. None of this is simple. Domestic squalor is dark and serious. It leaves behind guilt or sadness. Anger bestows on you a portrait of your soul. It is often followed by guilt. The portrait is more detailed if you have children.

I was driving the car in city traffic. In the back seat my two youngest daughters were whispering. I had picked them up at school for reasons I forget. The older one had been asked to baby-sit for a neighbor. It was her first job. It was her first time baby-sitting. She was eleven and her younger sister was nine. She was going across the street to a neighbor's house. I was to be on call in case there was any problem. She was excited and began to talk about how she would spend the fifty cents an hour she was going to be making. Suddenly the younger sister shrieked, "I want a baby-sitting job too. I am as responsible. I can do it. I should go with her." The older one said no, this was her job. I could hear the tremble in her voice. The younger one said yes, she was entitled. She should be baby-sitting too. She was shouting. She was not going to let the older one grow up faster, have a privilege ahead of her, take authority, make money. She was not going to be the baby in our family left behind as the others went out into the world. She sounded ferocious. The older one held firm. "This is my job. I am old enough, not you." I felt squeezed. The older one had a right to be older. She had a right to grow up first. The younger one had a right to object, to be hurt, to scramble to keep up. The older one was white as ash when I glanced in the mirror. The younger one was red and there were tears in her eyes. I made a decision. "No," I said, "baby-sitting is a one-person job and they asked your sister so she is going alone. She is the older sister," I said, announcing a fact that was always in dispute. The younger one collapsed in deep sobs. The older one was quiet in victory. The younger one said, "I want to die. I need to see a psychiatrist right away."

Then I was angry. This was manipulation, this was threat. This was playing on my nerves. "No," I said, "you don't need a psychiatrist. You aren't old enough to go baby-sitting and that's all."

"I can't stand my life," she said. "I don't care," I said. "Send me to a psychiatrist," she said between sobs. "Send yourself," I said. "I have no money," she wailed, "because you won't let me baby-sit," she added. "Too bad," I said. Later I worried. In preserving the right of the elder had I wounded the younger beyond repair? Did she need a psychiatrist? Why did ordinary rivalry and entitlement cause her such pain? Was that normal? Had I been cruel? Should I have forced the older one to share her grown-up moment with the younger? The scene plays over and over in my mind, half funny, half tragic, and each time it brings with it a feeling of futility, of helplessness. I know it sounds like nothing now, but then . . .

There is always the fear of death. When my children were young it came over me all the time. I could not bear to think of them grieving for me. I could not bear to think of them missing me. I was afraid to fly. From liftoff to touchdown I thought of them needing and not having a mother and I would imagine their loss in specific detail. The pain of it was quite extraordinary, especially since I was alive and all that loss was purely anticipated, conjured. In those days I would worry about car accidents, mutating cells, sudden strokes, slowly debilitating nerve diseases, all because I could not tolerate the idea of my children hurt the way my death would hurt them. As soon as they all became old enough so that my desire to survive had to be for reasons other than their urgent need I became a fearless flier, a person stoical about illness and ready if need be to let my life go. Relief is what I felt. My death had become my own again. The terror departed, or almost departed.

It returned whenever I thought something might happen to one of them.

This musing on death, my death, their death, was in part a product of anger, a way of punishing myself, a way of playing with a wound, a way of expressing the hard-to-express guilt.

Anna Freud said, "No child is wholly loved." She knew that in each sacred mother-and-child circle there is in addition to all the necessary well-touted tenderness a mutual anger, a mutual distaste that bides its time, holds its place, but bursts through now and then like a summer squall, hard and brief, startling, turning the leaves around on the branches and drenching the ground. The hostility a mother may feel for her children is natural enough, harmless enough, except in the cases of postpartum depression when the hormonal stew brews a malicious kind of toxin and mothers can actually harm their children, do fear harming their children, can themselves die under the effort to keep their rage contained. But the anger is there in diluted form in most mothers and in most babies. There is the baby's primordial fear and rage at the engulfing mother. We've all known babies to bite, scream, hit, pinch, grit their teeth and kick. The baby needs to be a separate self and pushes against the mother who holds him. The baby can't help but hate the mother who holds back the hand, who says no, who does not supply what is needed fast enough. The mother returns the sentiment. She may be enraged with loss of sleep. She may be mourning for her clipped wings, wanting her body back again for herself alone.

Maternal guilt. If there is too much anger there can be too much guilt. If there is too much guilt we can have trouble letting our children go off to explore the room, the school, the world. If we are too guilty we become frantic with the need to prove to ourselves and others what good mothers we really are. Most of us, feminist or traditional woman, at home or at work, manage to contain the small showers of maternal anger and guilt that are simply a part of normal weather conditions. Some of us do not.

I am working on a magazine article. I have left my two youngest daughters with my trusted housekeeper. The rain has been falling since noon. The buses moved slowly. I am late getting home. There is a silent heavy quiet on our block. The sound of water running down the drains, of cars suddenly braking, of the wind blowing mixes with the splashing of my feet in the puddles that gather in the slopes and heaves of our sidewalk. The older sister is playing with a friend. I see them in their room, a horse show, stuffed animals sitting in rows, sheets for curtains, pillows on the floor. I look for my youngest daughter. I can't find her. I call her name. I run up the stairs. I run down the stairs. I go into my bedroom. I see her small red sneaker. I open the door to my closet and there she is, curled up on the hard floor. Her face is stained with dirt. Her hair is tangled. She is as pale as an Edward Gorey character walking through a graveyard. Her older sister hadn't allowed her in the game. She was alone. She wanted to play too. She had nobody to play with. The sad story was told with full emotion, with bitten lip, with tears caught in her eyelashes.

I should have been home to read her a story. I should have been home to take her out in the rain to buy ice cream at the store. I should have been there to take her away when her sister closed the door. She felt like a waif, like an orphan, like a sisterless, motherless child. She was waiting in the closet for me to come home. I knew this was not the end of the world, that dramas like this are the stuff of childhood. Without knowing loneliness how can we be human? I knew that she would be all right, I knew that her older sister's friend would leave at the end of the afternoon and the younger one would be restored to her position as playmate of the hour. Still the stark, empty, dark look in the younger one's eyes made my stomach turn. I should have been there for her.

Later we played an endless game of Candyland. But I couldn't forget so easily. It was my responsibility to keep at bay the nightmares of childhood and I had failed: what is worse than being left out, hearing the whispers of sister and friend? I had made an unspoken, unthought-out promise, no fingers crossed, at the moment I conceived this wanted child that I would always be there, but of course I didn't mean all the time, I didn't mean day and night, and I had no way of knowing that it would rain and the buses would take so long and that her sister wouldn't let her play. So what harm was done? Yet the feeling stayed: What kind of mother is out pursuing her own fortune when her child is lying there on the closet floor?

This story, of my daughter on the closet floor, has remained in my mind for twenty years despite the fact that nothing extraordinary happened. Think, then, of the power to frighten a trusting parent that lies inside the nursery school. Think of the already guiltridden mother who drops her child off at her local day care center while through her mind run terrible pictures. What exactly is being done to her child in her absence? The imagination can run riot.

The social scientists tell us that it's all right to go back to work but the psychiatrists remind us how important attachment is, how the young child builds a separate self, how insecurity threatens the first steps toward independence, how sexual identity, future sexual pleasure are embedded in the toddler years. How could we not be guilty, how could we not feel guilty, no matter what we do. Someone is getting short shrift: most often that someone is ourselves.

The New Momism

Susan J. Douglas and Meredith W. Michaels

In this humorous and incisive excerpt, two mothers (both college professors) look at how media images of motherhood have become oppressive to everyday moms. I find their media criticism entertaining, insightful, and liberating.

~

IT'S 5:22 P.M. You're in the grocery checkout line. Your three-year-old is writhing on the floor, screaming, because you have refused to buy her a Teletubby pinwheel. Your six-year-old is whining, repeatedly, in a voice that could saw through cement, "But mommy, puleeze, puleeze" because you have not bought him the latest "Lunchables," which features, as the four food groups, Cheetos, a Snickers, Cheez Whiz, and Twizzlers. Your teenager, who has not spoken a single word in the past four days except, "You've ruined my life," followed by "Everyone else has one," is out in the car, sulking, with the new rap-metal band Piss on the Parentals blasting through the headphones of a Discman.

To distract yourself, and to avoid the glares of other shoppers who have already deemed you the worst mother in America, you leaf through *People* magazine. Inside, Uma Thurman gushes "Motherhood Is Sexy."[1] Moving on to *Good Housekeeping*, Vanna White says of her child, "When I hear his cry at six-thirty in the morning, I have a smile on my face, and I'm not an early riser."[2] Another unexpected source of earth-mother wisdom, the newly maternal Pamela Lee, also confides to *People*, "I just love getting up with him in the middle of the night to feed him or soothe him."[3] Brought back to reality by stereophonic whining, you indeed feel as sexy as Rush Limbaugh in a thong.

You drag your sorry ass home. Now, if you were a "good" mom, you'd joyfully empty the shopping bags and transform the process of putting the groceries away into a fun game your kids love to play (upbeat Raffi songs would provide a lilting soundtrack). Then, while you steamed the broccoli and poached the chicken breasts in Vouvray and Evian water, you and the kids would also be doing jigsaw puzzles in the shape of the United Arab Emirates so they learned some geography. Your cheerful teenager would say, "Gee, Mom, you gave me the best advice on that last homework assignment." When your husband arrives, he is so overcome with admiration for how well you do it all that he looks lovingly into your eyes, kisses you, and presents you with a diamond anniversary bracelet. He then announces that he has gone on flex time for the next two years so that he can split childcare with you fifty-fifty. The children, chattering away happily, help set the table, and then eat their broccoli. After dinner, you all go out and stencil the driveway with autumn leaves.

But maybe this sounds slightly more familiar. "I won't unpack the groceries! You can't make me," bellows your child as he runs to his room, knocking down a lamp on the way. "Eewee—gross out!"

he yells and you discover that the cat has barfed on his bed. You have fifteen minutes to make dinner because there's a school play in half an hour. While the children fight over whether to watch *Hot Couples* or people eating larvae on *Fear Factor,* you zap some Prego spaghetti sauce in the microwave and boil some pasta. *You* set the table. "Mommy, Mommy, Sam losted my hamster," your daughter wails. Your ex-husband calls to say he won't be taking the kids this weekend after all because his new wife, Buffy, twenty-three, has to go on a modeling shoot in Virgin Gorda for the *Sports Illustrated* swimsuit issue, and "she really needs me with her." You go to the TV room to discover the kids watching transvestites punching each other out on *Jerry Springer*. The pasta boils over and scalds the hamster, now lying prostrate on the floor with its legs twitching in the air. "Get your butts in here this instant or I'll murder you immediately," you shriek, by way of inviting your children to dinner. "I hate this pasta—I only like the kind shaped like wagon wheels!" "Mommy, you killded my hamster!"

If you're like us—mothers with an attitude problem—you may be getting increasingly irritable about this chasm between the ridiculous, honey-hued ideals of perfect motherhood in the mass media and the reality of mothers' everyday lives. And you may also be worn down by media images that suggest that however much you do for and love your kids, it is never enough. The love we feel for our kids, the joyful times we have with them, are repackaged into unattainable images of infinite patience and constant adoration so that we fear, as Kristin van Ogtrop put it movingly in *The Bitch in the House,* "I will love my children, but my love for them will always be imperfect."[4]

From the moment we get up until the moment we collapse in bed at night, the media are out there, calling to us, yelling, "Hey you! Yeah, you! Are you *really* raising your kids right?" Whether it's the cover of *Redbook* or *Parents* demanding "Are You a Sensitive Mother?" "Is Your Child Eating Enough?" "Is Your Baby Normal?" (and exhorting us to enter its pages and have great sex at 25, 35, or 85), the nightly news warning us about missing children, a movie trailer hyping a film about a cross-dressing dad who's way more fun than his stinky, careerist wife (*Mrs. Doubtfire*), or Dr. Laura telling some poor mother who works four hours a week that she's neglectful, the siren song blending seduction and accusation is there all the time. Mothers are subjected to an onslaught of beatific imagery, romantic fantasies, self-righteous sermons, psychological warnings, terrifying movies about losing their children, even more terrifying news stories about abducted and abused children, and totally unrealistic advice about how to be the most perfect and revered mom in the neighborhood, maybe even in the whole country. (Even *Working Mother*—which should have known better—had a "Working Mother of the Year Contest." When Jill Kirschenbaum became the editor in 2001, one of the first things she did was dump this feature, noting that motherhood should not be a "competitive sport.") We are urged to be fun-loving, spontaneous, and relaxed, yet, at the same time, scared out of our minds that our kids could be killed at any moment. No wonder 81 percent of women in a recent poll said it's harder to be a mother now than it was twenty or thirty years ago, and 56 percent felt mothers were doing a worse job today than mothers back then.[5] Even mothers who deliberately avoid TV and magazines, or who pride themselves on seeing through them, have trouble escaping the standards of perfection, and the sense of threat, that the media ceaselessly atomize into the air we breathe.

We are both mothers, and we adore our kids—for example,

neither one of us has ever locked them up in dog crates in the basement (although we have, of course, been tempted). The smell of a new baby's head, tucking a child in at night, receiving homemade, hand-scrawled birthday cards, heart-to-hearts with a teenager after a date, seeing *them* become parents—these are joys parents treasure. But like increasing numbers of women, we are fed up with the myth—shamelessly hawked by the media—that motherhood is eternally fulfilling and rewarding, that it is *always* the best and most important thing you do, that there is only a narrowly prescribed way to do it right, and that if you don't love each and every second of it there's something really wrong with you. At the same time, the two of us still have been complete suckers, buying those black-and-white mobiles that allegedly turn your baby into Einstein Jr., feeling guilty for sending in store-bought cookies to the class bake sale instead of homemade like the "good" moms, staying up until 2:30 A.M. making our kids' Halloween costumes, driving to the Multiplex 18 at midnight to pick up teenagers so they won't miss the latest outing with their friends. We know that building a scale model of Versailles out of mashed potatoes may not be quite as crucial to good mothering as *Martha Stewart Living* suggests. Yet here we are, cowed by that most tyrannical of our cultural icons, Perfect Mom. So, like the millions of women, we buy into these absurd ideals at the same time that we resent them and think they are utterly ridiculous and oppressive. After all, our parents—the group Tom Brokaw has labeled "the greatest generation"—had parents who whooped them on the behind, screamed stuff at them like "I'll tear you limb from limb," told them babies came from cabbage patches, never drove them four hours to a soccer match, and yet they seemed to have nonetheless saved the western world.

We see a rise in the media of what we call the "new momism":

the insistence that no woman is truly complete or fulfilled unless she has kids, that women remain the best primary caretakers of children, and that to be a remotely decent mother, a woman has to devote her entire physical, psychological, emotional, and intellectual being, 24/7, to her children. The new momism is a highly romanticized and yet demanding view of motherhood in which the standards for success are impossible to meet. The term "momism" was initially coined by the journalist Philip Wylie in his highly influential 1942 bestseller *Generation of Vipers,* and it was a very derogatory term. Drawing from Freud (who else?), Wylie attacked the mothers of America as being so smothering, overprotective, and invested in their kids, especially their sons, that they turned them into dysfunctional, sniveling weaklings, maternal slaves chained to the apron strings, unable to fight for their country or even stand on their own two feet.[6] We seek to reclaim this term, rip it from its misogynistic origins, and apply it to an ideology that has snowballed since the 1980s and seeks to return women to the Stone Age.

The "new momism" is a set of ideals, norms, and practices, most frequently and powerfully represented in the media, that seem on the surface to celebrate motherhood, but which in reality promulgate standards of perfection that are beyond your reach. The new momism is the direct descendant and latest version of what Betty Friedan famously labeled the "feminine mystique" back in the 1960s. The new momism *seems* to be much more hip and progressive than the feminine mystique, because now, of course, mothers can and do work outside the home, have their own ambitions and money, raise kids on their own, or freely choose to stay at home with their kids rather than being forced to. And unlike the feminine mystique, the notion that women should be subservient to men is not an accepted tenet of the new momism. Central to the new momism, in fact, is the feminist insistence that women have choices, that they are active agents in control of their own destiny, that they have autonomy. But here's where the distortion of feminism occurs. The only truly enlightened choice to make as a woman, the one that proves, first, that you are a "real" woman, and second, that you are a decent, worthy one, is to become a "mom" and to bring to child rearing a combination of selflessness and professionalism that would involve the cross cloning of Mother Teresa with Donna Shalala. Thus the new momism is deeply contradictory: It both draws from and repudiates feminism.

The fulcrum of the new momism is the rise of a really pernicious ideal in the late twentieth century that the sociologist Sharon Hays has perfectly labeled "intensive mothering."[7] It is no longer okay, as it was even during the heyday of June Cleaver, to let (or make) your kids walk to school, tell them to stop bugging you and go outside to play, or, God forbid, serve them something like Tang, once the preferred beverage of the astronauts, for breakfast. Of course many of our mothers baked us cookies, served as Brownie troop leaders, and chaperoned class trips to Elf Land. But today, the standards of good motherhood are really over the top. And they've gone through the roof at the same time that there has been a real decline in leisure time for most Americans.[8] The yuppie work ethic of the 1980s, which insisted that even when you were off the job you should be working—on your abs, your connections, your portfolio, whatever—absolutely conquered motherhood. As the actress Patricia Heaton jokes in *Motherhood & Hollywood*, now mothers are supposed to "sneak echinacea" into the "freshly squeezed, organically grown orange juice" we've made for our kids and teach them to "download research for their kindergarten report on 'My Family Tree—The Early Roman Years.'"[9]

Intensive mothering insists that mothers acquire professional-level skills such as those of a therapist, pediatrician ("Dr. Mom"), consumer products safety inspector, and teacher, and that they lavish every ounce of physical vitality they have, the monetary equivalent of the gross domestic product of Australia, and, most of all, every single bit of their emotional, mental, and psychic energy on their kids. We must learn to put on the masquerade of the doting, self-sacrificing mother and wear it at all times. With intensive mothering, everyone watches us, we watch ourselves and other mothers, and we watch ourselves watching ourselves. How many of you know someone who swatted her child on the behind in a supermarket because he was, say, opening a pack of razor blades in the toiletries aisle, only to be accosted by someone she never met who threatened to put her up on child-abuse charges? In 1997, one mother was arrested for child neglect because she left a ten-year-old and a four-year-old home for an hour and a half while she went to the supermarket.[10] Motherhood has become a psychological police state.

Intensive mothering is the ultimate female Olympics: We are all in powerful competition with each other, in constant danger of being trumped by the mom down the street, or in the magazine we're reading. The competition isn't just over who's a good mother—it's over who's the best. We compete with each other; we compete with ourselves. The best mothers always put their kids' needs before their own, period. The best mothers are the main caregivers. For the best mothers, their kids are the center of the universe. The best mothers always smile. They always understand. They are never tired. They never lose their temper. They never say, "Go to the neighbor's house and play while Mommy has a beer." Their love for their children is boundless, unflagging, flawless, total.

Mothers today cannot just respond to their kids' needs, they must predict them—and with the telepathic accuracy of Houdini. They must memorize verbatim the books of all the child-care experts and know which approaches are developmentally appropriate at different ages. They are supposed to treat their two-year-olds with "respect." If mothers screw up and fail to do this on any given day, they should apologize to their kids, because any misstep leads to permanent psychological and/or physical damage. Anyone who questions whether this is *the* best and *the* necessary way to raise kids is an insensitive, ignorant brute. This is just common sense, right?[11]

The new momism has become unavoidable, unless you raise your kids in a yurt on the tundra, for one basic reason: Motherhood became one of the biggest media obsessions of the last three decades, exploding especially in the mid-1980s and continuing unabated to the present. Women have been deluged by an ever-thickening mudslide of maternal media advice, programming, and marketing that powerfully shapes how we mothers feel about our relationships with our own kids and, indeed, how we feel about ourselves. These media representations have changed over time, cutting mothers some real slack in the 1970s, and then increasingly closing the vise in the late 1980s and after, despite important rebellions by Roseanne and others. People don't usually notice that motherhood has been such a major media fixation, revolted or hooked as they've been over the years by other media excesses like the O. J. Simpson trials, the Lewinsky-Clinton imbroglio, the Elian Gonzalez carnival, *Survivor,* or the 2002 Washington-area sniper killings in which "profilers" who knew as much as SpongeBob SquarePants nonetheless got on TV to tell us what the killer was thinking.

But make no mistake about it—mothers and motherhood came under unprecedented media surveillance in the 1980s and beyond.

And since the media traffic in extremes, in anomalies—the rich, the deviant, the exemplary, the criminal, the gorgeous—they emphasize fear and dread on the one hand and promote impossible ideals on the other. In the process, *Good Housekeeping People, E!,* Lifetime, *Entertainment Tonight,* and *NBC Nightly News* built an interlocking, cumulative image of the dedicated, doting "mom" versus the delinquent, bad "mother." There have been, since the early 1980s, several overlapping media frameworks that have fueled the new momism. First, the media warned mothers about the external threats to their kids from abductors and the like. Then the "family values" crowd made it clear that supporting the family was not part of the government's responsibility. By the late 1980s, stories about welfare and crack mothers emphasized the internal threats to children from mothers themselves. And finally, the media brouhaha over the "Mommy Track" reaffirmed that businesses could not or would not budge much to accommodate the care of children. Together, and over time, these frameworks produced a prevailing common sense that only you, the individual mother, are responsible for your child's welfare: The buck stops with you, period, and you'd better be a superstar.

Of course there has been a revolution in fatherhood over the past thirty years, and millions of men today tend to the details of child rearing in ways their own fathers rarely did. Feminism prompted women to insist that men change diapers and pack school lunches, but it also gave men permission to become more involved with their kids in ways they have found to be deeply satisfying. And between images of cuddly, New Age dads with babies asleep on their chests (think old Folger's ads), movies about hunky men and a baby (or clueless ones who shrink the kids), and sensational news stories about "deadbeat dads" and men who beat up their sons' hockey coaches, fathers too have been subject to a media "dad patrol." But it pales in comparison to the new momism. After all, a dad who knows the name of his kids' pediatrician and reads them stories at night is still regarded as a saint; a mother who doesn't is a sinner.

Once you identify it, you see the new momism everywhere. The recent spate of magazines for "parents" (i.e., mothers) bombard the anxiety-induced mothers of America with reassurances that they can (after a $100,000 raise and a personality transplant) produce bright, motivated, focused, fun-loving, sensitive, cooperative, confident, contented kids just like the clean, obedient ones on the cover. The frenzied hypernatalism of the women's magazines alone (and that includes *People, Us,* and *InStyle*), with their endless parade of perfect, "sexy" celebrity moms who've had babies, adopted babies, been to sperm banks, frozen their eggs for future use, hatched the frozen eggs, had more babies, or adopted a small Tibetan village, all to satisfy their "baby lust," is enough to make you want to get your tubes tied. (These profiles always insist that celebs all love being "moms" much, much more than they do their work, let alone being rich and famous, and that they'd spend every second with their kids if they didn't have that pesky blockbuster movie to finish.) Women without children, wherever they look, are besieged by ridiculously romantic images that insist that having children is the most joyous, fulfilling experience in the galaxy, and if they don't have a small drooling creature who likes to stick forks in electrical outlets, they are leading bankrupt, empty lives. Images of ideal moms and their miracle babies are everywhere, like leeches in the Amazon, impossible to dislodge and sucking us dry.

There is also the ceaseless outpouring of books on toilet training, separating one sibling's fist from another sibling's eye socket, expressing breast milk while reading a legal brief, helping pre-schoolers to "own" their feelings, getting Joshua to do his home-work, and raising teenage boys so they become Sensitive New Age Guys instead of rooftop snipers or Chippendale dancers. Over eight hundred books on motherhood were published between 1970 and 2000; only twenty-seven of these came out between 1970 and 1980, so the real avalanche happened in the past twenty years.[12] We've learned about the perils of "the hurried child" and "hyperparent-ing," in which we schedule our kids with so many enriching activi-ties that they make the secretary of state look like a couch spud. But the unhurried child probably plays too much Nintendo and is out in the garage building pipe bombs, so you can't underschedule them either.

Then there's the Martha Stewartization of America, in which we are meant to sculpt the carrots we put in our kids' lunches into the shape of peonies and build funhouses for them in the backyard; this has raised the bar to even more ridiculous levels than during the June Cleaver era. Most women know that there was a massive public relations campaign during World War II to get women into the workforce, and then one right after the war to get them to go back to the kitchen. But we haven't fully focused on the fact that another, more subtle, sometimes unintentional, more long-term propaganda campaign began in the 1980s to redomesticate the women of America through motherhood.[13] Why aren't all the mothers of America leaning out their windows yelling "I'm mad as hell and I'm not going to take it anymore"?

The new momism involves more than just impossible ideals about child rearing. It redefines all women, first and foremost, through their relationships to children. Thus, being a citizen, a worker, a governor, an actress, a First Lady, all are supposed to take a back seat to motherhood. (Remember how people questioned whether Hillary Clinton was truly maternal because she had only one child?) By insisting that being a mother—and a perfect one at that—is the most important thing a woman can do, a prerequisite for being thought of as admirable and noble, the new momism insists that if you want to do anything else, you'd better prove first that you're a doting, totally involved mother before proceeding. This is not a requirement for men. The only recourse for women who want careers, or to do anything else besides stay home with the kids all day, is to prove that they can "do it all." As the feminist writer (and pioneer) Letty Cottin Pogrebin put it, "You can go be a CEO, and a good one, but if you're not making a themed birthday party, you're not a good mother," and, thus, you are a failure."[14]

The new momism has evolved over the past few decades, becoming more hostile to mothers who work, and more insistent that all mothers become ever more closely tethered to their kids. The mythology of the new momism now insinuates that, when all is said and done, the enlightened mother chooses to stay home with the kids. Back in the 1950s, mothers stayed home because they had no choice, so the thinking goes (even though by 1955 more mothers were working than ever before). Today, having been to the office, having tried a career, women supposedly have seen the inside of the male working world and found it to be the inferior choice to staying home, especially when their kids' future is at stake. It's not that mothers can't hack it (1950s thinking). It's that progressive mothers refuse to hack it. Inexperienced women thought they knew what they wanted, but they got experience and learned they were wrong. Now mothers have seen the error of their ways, and supposedly seen that the June Cleaver model, if taken as a *choice,* as opposed to a requirement, is the truly modern, fulfilling, forward-thinking version of motherhood.

In the 1960s, women, and especially young women, were surrounded by mixed messages, one set telling them that there was a new day dawning, they were now equal to men and could change the world, the other telling them they were destined to be housewives, were subservient to men, and could never achieve equality. Electrified by the civil rights and antiwar movements and their demands for freedom and participatory democracy, women could no longer stand being pulled in opposite directions, and opted for equality. Of course, the contradictions in our lives did not vanish—in the wake of the women's movement we were supposed to be autonomous, independent, accomplished, yet poreless, slim, nurturing, and deferential to men.[15] In the early twenty-first century, we see a mirror image of the 1960s, but without the proud ending: The same contradictions are there, but now the proposed resolution, like a mist in the culture, is for women to give up their autonomy and find peace and fulfillment in raising children.

In other words, ladies, the new momism seeks to contain and, where possible, eradicate, all of the social changes brought on by feminism. It is backlash in its most refined, pernicious form because it insinuates itself into women's psyches just where we have been rendered most vulnerable: in our love for our kids. The new momism, then, is deeply and powerfully political. The new momism is the result of the combustible intermixing of right-wing attacks on feminism and women, the media's increasingly finely tuned and incessant target marketing of mothers and children, the collapse of governmental institutions—public schools, child welfare programs—that served families in the past (imperfectly, to be sure), and mothers' own, very real desires to do the best job possible raising their kids in a culture that praises mothers in rhetoric and reviles them in public policy.

Plenty of mothers aren't buying this retro version of motherhood, although it works to make them feel very guilty and stressed. They want and need their own paychecks, they want and need adult interaction during the day, they want and need their own independence, and they believe—and rightly so—that women who work outside the home can be and are very good mothers to their kids. Other mothers don't want or need these things for the time being, or ever, and really would rather stay home. The question here is not which path women choose, or which one is "right." The question is why one reactionary, normative ideology, so out of sync with millions of women's lives, seems to be getting the upper hand.

Each of us, of course, has her own individual history as a mother, her own demons and satisfactions, her own failures and goals. But motherhood is, in our culture, emphasized as such an individual achievement, something you and you alone excel at or screw up. So it's easy to forget that motherhood *is* a collective experience. We want to erase the amnesia about motherhood—we *do* have a common history, it does tie us together, and it has made us simultaneously guilt-ridden and ready for an uprising. Let's turn the surveillance cameras away from ourselves and instead turn them on the media that shaped us and that manufactured more of our beliefs and practices than we may appreciate, or want to admit.

Especially troubling about all this media fare is the rise of even more impossible standards of motherhood today than those that tyrannized us in the past. For women in their twenties and thirties, the hypernatalism of the media promotes impossibly idealized expectations about motherhood (and fatherhood!) that may prove depressingly disappointing once junior arrives and starts throwing mashed beets on the wall. Peggy Orenstein reported in her 2000 book *Flux* that by the 1990s, "motherhood supplanted marriage as the source of romantic daydreams" for childless, unmarried women in their twenties and early to mid-thirties. To put it another way, "Motherhood has become increasingly central to women's conception of femininity, far more so than marriage." The women she talked to "believed children would answer basic existential questions of meaning" and would "provide a kind of unconditional love that relationships with men did not." They over-idealized motherhood and bought into the norm of "the Perfect Mother—the woman for whom childbearing supersedes all other identities and satisfactions."[16] A new generation of young women, for whom the feminine mystique is ancient history, and who haven't experienced what it took for women to fight their way out of the kitchen, may be especially seduced by media profiles suggesting that if Reese Witherspoon can marry young and become an A-list actress while raising a three-year-old and expecting another child, then you can "do it all" too. Just as Naomi Wolf, Susan Faludi, and Camryn Manheim sought to get women to say "excuuuse me" to the size-zero ideal, we would like women to just say no to the new momism.

Finally, this essay is a call to arms. With so many smart, hard-working, dedicated, tenacious, fed-up women out there, can't we all do a better job of talking back to the media that hector us all the time? As we get assaulted by "15 Ways to Stress Proof Your Child," "Boost Your Kid's Brainpower in Just 25 Minutes," "Discipline Makeover: Better Behavior in 21 Days," and "What It Really Takes to Make Your Baby Smarter," not to mention "The Sex Life You Always Wanted—How to Have it *Now*" (answer: put the kids up for adoption), let's develop, together, some really good comebacks.

And let's also take a second look at these "wars" we're supposed to be involved with: the "war" against welfare mothers, the "war" between working versus stay-at-home mothers. While these wars do often benefit one set of mothers over another, what they do best is stage *all* mothers' struggles, in the face of the most pathetic public policies for women and children in the western world, as a catfight. Then the politicians who've failed to give us decent day care or maternity leave can go off and sip their sherry while mothers point fingers at each other. Our collective dilemmas as mothers are always translated into individual issues that each of us has to confront by herself, alone, with zero help. These media frameworks that celebrate the rugged individualism of mothers, then, justify and reinforce public policies (or lack thereof) that make it harder to be a mother in the United States than in any other industrialized society.

As mothers, we appreciate all too well how much time and attention children need and deserve, and how deeply committed we become to our kids. We can be made to cry at the drop of a hat by a Hallmark commercial or a homemade Mother's Day card. We get roped into the new momism because we do feel that our society is not providing our kids with what they need. But the problem with the new momism is that it insists that there is one and only one way the children of America will get what they need: if mom provides it. If dad "pitches in," well, that's just an extra bonus. The government? Forget it.

We fear that, today, we have a new common sense about motherhood that may be as bad, or worse, as the one that chained mothers to their Maytags in 1957. It wasn't always like this. There was a time in the now distant past when there was something called the Women's Liberation Movement. They are the folks who brought you "the personal is political." Enough lies have been told by Pat Robertson, Rush Limbaugh, and others about what feminists said about motherhood and children to fill a Brazilian landfill center. But when we exhume what feminists really hoped to change about motherhood, hopes buried under a slag heap of cultural amnesia and backlash, the rise of the new momism seems like the very last set of norms you would predict would conquer motherhood in America in the early twenty-first century. Let's go back to a time when many women felt free to tell the truth about motherhood—e.g., that at times they felt ambivalent about it because it was so hard and yet so undervalued—and when women sought to redefine how children were raised so that it wasn't only women who pushed strollers, played Uncle Wiggly, or quit their jobs once kids arrived. Of course these women loved their kids. But were they supposed to give up everything for them? Are we?

Anyhow, the next time you read about Sarah Jessica Parker's perfect marriage and motherhood, don't sigh and say, "Oh, I wish that was my life." Instead, say, "Give me a break." (Or, alternatively, "Give me a %$#$% break." Of course, most of you probably already say that.) Because, you know, if we all refuse to be whipsawed between these age-old poles of perfect and failed motherhood, designed to police us all, then we—all of us—get a break. And that, you see, was what feminists were asking for in the first place.

NOTES

1. *People,* September 21, 1998.
2. *Good Housekeeping,* January 1995.
3. *People,* July 8, 1996.
4. Kristin van Ogtrop, "Attila the Honey I'm Home," *The Bitch in the House* (New York: William Morrow, 2002), p. 169.

5. "Motherhood Today—A Tougher Job, Less Ably Done," The Pew Research Center for the People & the Press, March 1997.

6. Philip Wylie, *Generation of Vipers* (New York: Holt, Rinehart and Winston, 1942). See also Ruth Feldstein's excellent discussion of momism in *Motherhood in Black and White: Race and Sex in American Liberalism, 1930–1965* (Ithaca: Cornell University Press, 2000), especially chapter 2.

7. Hays's book is must reading for all mothers, and we are indebted to her analysis of intensive mothering, from which this discussion draws. Sharon Hays, *The Cultural Contradictions of Motherhood* (New Haven: Yale University Press, 1996), p. 4.

8. For an account of the decline in leisure time see Juliet B. Schorr, *The Overworked American* (New York: Basic Books, 1992).

9. Patricia Heaton, *Motherhood & Hollywood* (New York: Villard Books, 2002), pp. 48–49.

10. See Katha Pollitt's terrific piece "Killer Moms, Working Nannies" in *The Nation,* November 24, 1997, p. 9.

11. Hays, pp. 4–9.

12. Based on an On-line Computer Library Center, Inc., search under the word *motherhood,* from 1970–2000.

13. Susan Faludi, in her instant classic *Backlash,* made this point, too, but the book focused on the various and multiple forms of backlash, and we will be focusing only on the use of motherhood here.

14. Interview, Letty Cottin Pogrebin, February 2001.

15. See Susan J. Douglas, *Where the Girls Are* (New York: Times Books, 1994), ch. 1.

16. Peggy Orenstein, *Flux: Women on Sex, Work, Love, Kids and Life in a Half-Changed World* (New York: Doubleday, 2000), pp. 105–6.

Power Moms and the Problem of Overparenting

Joan K. Peters

The standards of motherhood seem to have changed dramatically since we were kids. These days a "good mother" is expected to know just about everything: the latest in child psychology, safety equipment, nutrition, education. Many of us also feel pressure to expose our children to all forms of enrichment from the earliest possible age. My own mother looks on all this with a kind of quiet amusement. "We just didn't go to all this trouble," she'll sometimes say. In this excerpt, Joan Peters insightfully explores the current trend of "overparenting" and points out its drawbacks.

~

THE FEMINISTS OF THE SIXTIES and seventies rejected the Donna Reed model of womanhood. Many of their daughters, rejecting in turn the feminist model, have become "power moms" or "super-moms." Power moms may have been sales reps or run companies before their children were born; now, cell-phones in hand, they run their homes. Super-moms can spend the day trading bonds or processing words, but they still preside over their homes, making birthday cakes and Halloween costumes even if it takes staying up all night. Believing themselves to be the equals of men, and their motherwork to be more important than any job, these new moms hardly identify with that icon of domesticity who never troubled her pretty little head with bottom lines. They resemble her nonetheless.

Donna Reed, we should remember, was a power mom in her own right. Her motherhood was all-important; indeed, it was all of life. With her starched apron and her sunny equanimity, she not only embodied America's postwar hope but washed away the horrifying memory of the Depression, the war, and the Holocaust. Reduced to the borders of her circumscribed life, the world seemed a tame and welcoming place. Thus, in its collective imagination, America fled from the harsh world of men into the satiny arms of its good women. Father may have known best, but Americans loved Lucy, married Joan, and remembered Mama.

Although we today have hardly suffered the traumas of the first half of the century, we have had serious societal distress resulting from the war in Vietnam, the civil rights and youth movements, and steady economic decline. Women, who for the first time had thrust themselves into the midst of the harsh world, now seem to be considering a retreat to home. Raising high the banner of motherhood, many are once again trying to make children the center and goal of their lives. Never mind that *The Feminine Mystique* put the lie to the myth of the happy housewife; a surprising number of young women today have convinced themselves to try it again. But with a twist.

Since Donna Reed's lack of worldliness hardly appeals to

women raised "to be free to be you and me," they have remade her housewifery in their own image. Employed or not, today's women who choose traditional motherhood bring to it all the science, management, and goal orientation usually applied to work. Thus, they have preserved Donna Reed motherhood by appending worldly functions to it. To be fair, society's broader neglect of children has made raising them more time-consuming. In this respect, professionalizing motherhood is also a necessary adaptation to the increasing complexity of our lives. However, both these private and social responses seem suspiciously driven by our guilty impulse to placate the gods of patriarchy, who have become increasingly upset with women these days. As a result, rather than adapting motherhood to women's new lives, Americans have turned motherhood into a job.

OVERPARENTING: A PECULIARLY AMERICAN INVENTION

For the white middle class, the edifice of motherhood has ironically grown more massive as more mothers work outside the home. While the time available for mothering has shrunk by at least eight hours a day (plus commuting time), the job description has expanded to include ever more exacting functions. Mothers are now expected to be creative playmates, child development experts, and education specialists. Many I know practically run their children's schools. Some volunteer to teach French and computer science, do lunchroom duty, or raise funds for services and supplies no longer provided by hard-pressed school boards. And with many towns grown too dangerous for children to travel by bicycle, mothers must drive them to music lessons, hockey practice, and the Saturday matinee.

This intensive kind of motherhood is a recent, and uniquely American, creation. In the fifties—despite television's sentimentalization of motherhood—mothers were expected to take care of children and rear them, a task that usually involved keen attention to food, clothing, shelter, manners, and morals. Though some mothers headed Scout troops, played catch, and enjoyed an occasional game of Monopoly, motherhood did not necessarily include one-on-one play. Nor did PTA membership entail raising money for half the school budget. While parents may have exacted high grades, clean living, and religious observance from children, those standards were laid down without a great deal of hand-wringing about the proper way to raise a child.

In his memoir of growing up African American in the fifties, Nathan McCall sums up what for many people (including me) characterized family life, and therefore motherhood:

> My folks were typical of their generation of parents. They didn't focus much on us unless we were sick or had done something wrong. They didn't hold conversations with us. Love was understood rather than expressed, and values were transmitted by example, not word of mouth.

Of course, it is wonderful that we give so much more thought to raising children, but there may be a point of diminishing returns—for parents and children both. Today middle-class parents read books on toddler development, attend parent workshops, and learn how to talk so children will listen. They often treat applications to preschool with the reverence once reserved for applying to

Harvard. It's a rare mother who now unthinkingly tells children to "go out and play." Even in safe communities, most parents are more comfortable setting up a project for the child or having an outing together.

At one time parents heard a bit about their children's social life at the dinner table. Now we have closely monitored play groups, play dates, and quality time. Parents used to feel sufficiently dutiful signing a child's report card and coming in for the annual parent-teacher conference. Now mothers are involved in every aspect of their child's daily homework from online research to laser-perfect execution. In my daughter's public school, mothers learn the new math in order to help their children, and they take positions on the way writing is taught. When I was growing up, children's grades disappointed or pleased parents. Today parents grade themselves according to their children's performance.

Super-parenting has become so much the norm in America that most Americans do not find it aberrant. However, foreigners observing American parenting mores often find it bewilderingly excessive. One mother I interviewed offers a revealing view from abroad. As a widely published writer and a mother of four, she is a particularly astute observer; having graduated from an American college, lived in several American cities, and married an American, her view is an intimate one.

GIOCONDA BELLI

Gioconda Belli, a Nicaraguan novelist and poet who held several important public positions in her country, became the mother of her fourth child, Adriana, after moving to Los Angeles with her second husband, an American, in 1990. With daughters in graduate school and college and a son in high school, she was quickly initiated into American parenting.

What surprised her initially were her son Camilo's high school friends, who seemed angry and alienated from their parents. Camilo, by contrast, is very close to his parents and stepparents, typically participating in their social activities and often taking care of his baby sister and any other younger children in their home. His older sister Maryam took a job in Los Angeles to be near her family after receiving her degree in architecture. Melissa, the second daughter, visits during nearly every vacation from medical school.

Gioconda wondered why such closeness should be less typical for American children. Why do they routinely move away from home after college and often reject or rebel against their parents? Why do they distrust their parents?

When we meet to discuss these questions one morning, the beguiling Gioconda, famous for her passionate love poems, is dressed in what I've come to think of as her elegant gypsy style: a long flared skirt, colorful vest, bangles, and earrings that bob beneath a river of auburn ringlets. Sitting in the walled garden of her Spanish-style home, her toddler dashing over for periodic hugs, she tells me that her experience with her two-year-old has given her some insight into the teenage alienation that shocked her at first.

"Even at Gymboree," she says, "I notice how parents are so worried about the most minute details in the child's life—whether they had enough free versus structured time, for example. Or whether their child is participating with the group. The director of a prospective preschool reflected that same preoccupation when she assured us that they didn't have any Disney books, only 'good' books at their school.

"Here, parents discuss these things as if they were going to have a profound effect on their children, with a concern that seems disproportionate considering that children grow up exposed to all kinds of influences. Whether they have Disney books or not, the children come to school with their Simba lunch boxes and their Mickey Mouse sweatshirts. Yet the parents still worry so."

Listening to her thickly accented English, I am reminded that when I first met her a decade before in Nicaragua, Gioconda had brought the then-ten-year-old Camilo with her to the garden of my hotel for our interview about her country's dire political situation. And there he sat or roamed—without toys, crayons, entertainment, or our attention—for a full two hours. Being an American, I finally found some paper and pencils "to keep him busy." In her Los Angeles home, I comment that although I wasn't a parent myself at that time, I had been surprised, and somewhat anxious, that she had left Camilo to his own devices.

"Exactly," she continues. "To me, American parents seem to regard their children as so vulnerable that they must constantly protect them. Most Latins I know rather trust in a child's basic humanity. We don't want to shield them. If something isn't perfect, or time isn't arranged for them, the child will know that life isn't perfect. If they don't learn this, then they cannot engage themselves without our help. American children are rarely left to their own devices when they are small." She gathered herself up and leaned forward, very nearly leaping, as it were, to the heart of the matter.

"The concept of 'being there' for a child is, in my opinion, taken to an extreme in this country. It forces the parent to respond to the child in a very premeditated way that's not natural or spontaneous. So many parents here seem to feel as if they must react to *everything* the child does, as if being distracted or involved in something else while they are with him will harm the child. They are very anxious around their children, and one can almost feel, in their response to the child, the effort they have to make to pretend that they are delighted by any little thing.

"I personally think children can see through this and often get frustrated because, even though they know they don't have the parent's attention, there is the pretense that they do so they feel somehow cheated. It probably ends up also being exhausting and taking a lot of pleasure out of the relationship for the parent.

"I think it creates a more honest behavior pattern in the parent-child relationship and builds trust when a child knows that he or she cannot have the parents' attention all the time, that the parents also have to think of other things and do other things, or simply that sometimes they are just not in the mood. Forced involvement has to end up creating hostility, both for the parent that has to pretend and for the child that feels drawn into this game of pretense.

"Adrianita," she calls out to her daughter, who is now leaning down to pick up a muddy stick, "no, that's dirty." Adriana considers the injunction, then scurries off for the hose instead, using the water slowly dripping from its spout to clean her stick. The garden has neither a swing set nor a playhouse. "I think it's very hard for American parents," Gioconda continues, returning her gaze to me. "They have so many tasks. Child-rearing is like another profession: knowing the right mobile to buy for the infant's crib, the right music to play, which experts to read. The spontaneity of parenting is turned into a dreadful obligation. Such a preoccupation with children doesn't seem to me to be good for the children either. It takes away from children's *self*-importance, from their ability to take responsibility for their own happiness."

When the baby-sitter arrives, an aging Nicaraguan woman who begins at once to coo at Adriana, squatting to meet her eye to eye, we leave the garden for Gioconda's home office, a tiny "tower" room just big enough for her desk and two chairs. The manuscript of the German translation of her latest novel sits on her desk festooned with yellow Post-Its. I have read all three of her novels. All the protagonists are women; none, I realize, are mothers. Well, one does eventually have a child, but the novel centers on her premothering years.

When the new novel is published, Gioconda tells me, she'll have to go on a publicity tour for three weeks. It's longer than she wants to be away from Adriana, but she must go. Such a long time, I comment. But she reassures me that Adriana has her father, her siblings, her baby-sitter. "She will cope," she says. "That's part of what I'm talking about. American parents seem to think that children learn to cope later in life rather than in early childhood. They don't give their small children responsibility. Then when the children reach adolescence, parents expect them to suddenly become responsible. These children go from being the sun in a family to being a planet orbiting around it, and they are full of resentment."

Middle-class Latin family life is quite different from the American way, she explains. "I never thought that children were the center of my life, but that they participated in my life. I felt they had to learn to be the center of their own lives. I wanted them to understand that, although we were together in life, each of us was separate and responsible for our own lives. The same way I understood they had to separate from me, they had to understand I had to separate from them. I wanted them to know that in order to nourish them spiritually I had to have spiritual nourishment."

How does that different focus play itself out in daily parenting? I wonder out loud. "Take the subject of school," she offers. "I participated in my children's schools, offering a poetry workshop or something, so I would know their friends and teachers, but I didn't supervise their work. Although I helped if they asked, I never did homework with my children. I see American parents obsessing about homework and taking over a teenager's college application process, as if where the child goes is a reflection of the child's worth. I fear that for American parents it is.

"In the States children are made to feel that their worth is going to be measured by the kind of college they get accepted to. This turns the college application process into judgment day, a judgment day that somehow will also reflect upon the parents, which makes the whole issue an agony for the teenager. It is as if the teenager bears the burden of proving to the world that her parents have done a good job of raising her. But the parents' intrusion and worry is such an emotional weight for the child that she withdraws just to protect herself. Teenagers here almost have to reject their parents in order to find themselves because the parents don't trust them to do it.

"Instead of controlling my children, I tried to create an intimacy with them. I've tried to parent while staying true to myself. We always had long talks about their feelings and mine. Even with Adriana, who is two, I talk about anger, sadness, and love in as grown-up a way as I can. I tell her if I don't want to play because I'm tired, sad, or feeling bad. I tell Camilo and my daughters about problems I have with work or with my husband so they know what life is. They are concerned about my life, and they don't hesitate to come to me with their problems. Even their American friends talk over their problems with my husband and me. They know we will help without overwhelming their own ideas or experience."

What is so striking about Gioconda's motherhood is how relaxed she is about parenting while still being very present with her children, how confident in sharing motherwork with her husband, her older children, and her baby-sitter, how she doesn't grade herself on her children's accomplishments. What is so striking about our American parenting style, after speaking with her, is our anxiety and constant supervision of children.

MOTHERHOOD WITH A HUMAN FACE

Once I asked the twenty-year-old daughter of dear friends what child-rearing advice she would give me. I asked her because she and her parents have an enviable relationship, and because she was so much herself and so comfortable in the world. "Break all the rules," she said unhesitatingly. Even before she explained, I knew what she meant.

When she was six, her parents took her out of school and together they traveled for several months through Mexico in a van. When she was seven, they left her with close friends for a month so they could each travel alone and rediscover their separate selves, as they put it. For several years she lived in a commune where all the adults, including her parents, shared parenting.

Were they good parents? The best I've ever known well. They were entirely themselves, yet responsible to their daughter. Their relationship with her was intimate, honest, and full of mutual delight—and still is. Not long ago they stopped to see us after spending a month with their daughter in Uruguay, where she studies political science at the university. She served as their translator when they lectured there at a professional gathering. Rather than stay in a hotel, they put up with sleeping bags on the floor of her unheated apartment in order to get to know her daily life, her roommate, and her friends. Midway through their stay, they took her and a friend skiing for a week. On the eve of their departure, their daughter's friends threw a party for them and each brought a small gift. That, we all agreed, was a parent's dream.

Breaking all the rules means living in your own skin in the life you want—with your child. Being exactly who you are and helping your children to be themselves is the kind of mothering that lends itself to the growth of self and soul for both parents and child.

The novelist Kate Braverman says of her daughter: "She's not like me—addicted to the brutal, dark night skies—she's a sunny, amiable child. I find it curious how she's turned out. I've raised her so unconventionally. This child has literally grown up at poetry readings. We lived in the jungle without electricity for a year in Maui. I've raised her as the daughter of a poet, and I must say she's flourished."

Notice that Braverman never tried to be the sunny, amiable mother of the myth. But she was always a nurturing mother. A self-described maniacally driven writer, she also knows "that there are times when I am going to lose a scene or a story because I choose to let my daughter have that moment. I recognize that there are moments when motherhood will take precedence over sitting at my computer." This is not the cold careerist or the distracted genius who neglects her daughter. Braverman values having a child but did not turn into someone else when she became a mother.

Maintaining self while nurturing involves more than simply cultivating your independent life and living the way you want. It also takes a kind of honesty that the American maternal ideal does not encourage. The psychologist Kathy Weingarten says that we don't tell our children the truth about ourselves because we are afraid of that dangerous nonmaternal self—the one that puts herself first, that, on occasion, feels sad, angry, ambivalent. We censor constantly to project the image of the ideal mother. When Weingarten discovered that she had cancer and decided she had no choice but to put herself first, her mothering changed forever. Once she told her children the truth about her illness and her feelings, she decided never to go back to living the mother myth because she has "a better life now, one in which more of the time, I do more of what I want, and believe I am a good mother for it."

Can we really talk to children? Can we tell them about our day, truly? Are we too sanitized, Disneyized, and dominated by our own parents' belief in the separation of child and adult spheres? Growing up, no one I knew had any idea about their parents' incomes, illnesses, or emotional lives. We guessed, but we were almost always wrong, misconstruing their frustrations as anger at us, their personal disappointments as indifference.

Mary Gordon wrote a novella about an incident at the beach when, for a split second, thinking she and her daughter had been pulled too far out by the undertow, she saw that she was about to save herself first. Is this the awful truth mothers spare their children? Would children be horrified to know that even mothers have an instinct for self-preservation? Or would telling the truth perhaps simply make mothers more human, and children more accepting of their own frailties?

When parents do not violate their true selves after they have children, they are more available and more authentic with their children. In this regard, children of even flawed parents who break the rules have an advantage over children raised in homes where people parent according to the flawed ideal of self-sacrificing motherhood. The latter may often look perfect but be emotionally tense with resentments. How could it not be so if women violate their training, their ambitions, and themselves when they become mothers?

Claiming the Joy

Daphne de Marneffe

Balancing work and family is a persistent challenge. Work is an economic necessity for many women, and it is often also a deeply felt need. Still, the need to work conflicts with a basic, passionate instinct to mother our children, and so mothers often feel pulled in two directions. In this essay, Daphne de Marneffe, a psychologist and mother of three, explores this fundamental conflict with remarkable freshness and insight. Above all, she asks: What prevents us from taking pleasure in motherhood, even with all its tensions and challenges?

∼

WHEN OUR THIRD CHILD was born, it was June. He was a big baby, but he was my first easy birth. He was heavy, and for weeks I'd felt as if he might simply drop out of me. I fretted over the countless possible circumstances of his coming, about where I might be when it started, and with whom, since our second child had come eight minutes after we arrived at the hospital, and could well have been born in the car. But in the end, there was no rush. The baby remained securely settled till his due date. I was four centimeters dilated, and had been for days, when we decided to break my waters. The grandparents had long since arrived, and my husband was able to leave work unhurried. So, at noon on a cloudless spring day, he and I found ourselves driving to the hospital, nervous and almost shy to be alone again with this rite of passage before us, knowing that no words could make a bridge between this luminous, ordinary moment and the fruition, so near at hand, of the deep bloody marriage of our bodies.

That summer, I was happier than I had ever been in my life. I felt calmly ecstatic, in a place of lively rest. Was this the peace that came of having ridden the anxieties and strains and excitements of my fertility and having arrived safely at the other side? I felt light and heavy in my body at the same time, akin to the repose of sated passion. Yet my state of being was more continuous, less drowsy, and more alert. I felt I had satisfied my passion with the universe. We were content with each other; we'd done well.

During the first days of my son's life, while relatives were still there to entertain the older children, I read *The Leopard* while I nursed. It is a book of exquisite melancholy, the story of a magnetic Sicilian prince whose waning years coincide with the twilight of southern Italy's monarchic rule. Di Lampedusa wrote his novel in the last two years of his life, and his descriptions of the parched, unforgiving earth, of the nonchalant cruelties that pass for love, of the prince's last wisps of consciousness, are the product of a mind on intimate terms with life and death. On a still morning when everyone else went down to the park, I sat alone with the baby, listening to his newborn breaths as he slept on my lap and later his snuffling, hungry sucks. I could hear the cooing of the mourning dove perched on the telephone wire above the street, and the crows' cawing farther down the hill. Out the window were drooping sunlit

spider webs the children would later inspect and destroy, and but-
terflies, whose darting, bright lives are measured in days. I could
not have been more full; life could not have been more sweet. And
at the same time, there was also that ache, at "the rustling of the
grains of sand as they slid lightly away,"[1] and at my baby's sleeping
breath; that ache of beauty and longing and time and the unbearable fragility and surpassing preciousness of this moment.

Perhaps because I felt full, I could bear to gaze at the naked
contours of my yearning. This yearning had no object, at least no
visible, earthly one. I have heard it called "the nostalgia for the
present." There is the well-known biblical passage from 1 Corinthians: "For now we see through a glass, darkly; but then face to
face: now I know in part; but then shall I know even as also I am
known."[2] The words capture the expectant yearning, the urge to see
behind the veil, which seems to be part of the very fabric of love.
When we love, we are never spent, there is always more. Love seems
to encompass a feeling of seeking but of never quite reaching. Its
yearning is like a question with no final answer; to love life, to love
other people, it seems, is to tenderly embrace that question.

There were several things that made the time with my children over
that summer and the year that followed so happy. For one, I was
able to give myself over to it. After the roller coaster of my three
maternity leaves and a move, my clinical practice had diminished
by attrition. Though we didn't know what the future would bring,
in the short term, while we had an infant and two small children,
we could afford to live on one salary. As I am a psychologist, my
independent interests also lay in the same direction as parenthood.
I felt grounded and constructive when responding to the children's
needs and desires, in the countless acts of diapering, feeding, filling

cups, fastening shoes, comforting, and answering questions. One source of pleasure was doing different things while in each other's company. I liked reading a book while I was nursing the baby, while the five-year-old was drawing in another room and the two-year-old was pretending to be Prince Philip falling off his horse or building with blocks somewhere near my feet. I felt integrated in those moments—physically engaged with the baby, intellectually engaged with my book, emotionally engaged with my son and daughter and, of course, with the baby and the book, in harmony with everything around me and with life.

At home with the children I made sacrifices, but I did not sacrifice myself. I was one of the personalities, one of the players. We all had our wills, and we all loved one another. How would we make this work? Sometimes I played with them. Sometimes I took care of the household, cooking, cleaning, and dealing with the constant mound of paperwork. Sometimes I read a book, an activity that could feel as absorbing to me as they were. Sometimes they pulled the book out of my hand and said, "Stop reading!" and sometimes they went off and got lost in their own fantasy play.

As sleep deprivation once more receded and professional engagement returned as a valued goal, I felt increasingly compelled to focus my intellectual effort on understanding the most central thing in my life, taking care of children. My decision to write about it was possible because my husband was able and willing to support the family, and it was satisfying because it gave me a way to integrate my life as a psychologist and my life as a mother. Its chief advantage was that it allowed me to pursue my goals—to have time with the children, to engage in intellectual work, and eventually to make an income—in a way that helped me cope with the feeling of being pulled in different directions by my children and my work.

My particular solution to the dilemma of children and work is obviously not available, or attractive, to everyone. But the basic issues it was intended to address in my own life are central to many mothers' lives. Mothers everywhere want more freedom to be responsive to their children; they want the enormous importance of their nurturing to be acknowledged; and they suffer when they are unable to put together an arrangement that satisfies both their economic and psychological need for employment and their sense of the value of caring for children.

Women thinkers a generation before me, blessed like me with education and opportunity, cogently anatomized mothers' oppressions. Adrienne Rich, though she gestured toward the transformative potential of maternal pleasure, trained the force of her analysis on its corruption by patriarchal culture. My own experience drew me to charting the pleasures of caring for babies and small children, the very aspect of motherhood that Rich had intermittently found so painful. Certainly the realm of maternal pleasure is much wider than that; some mothers find their keenest delight in conversation with their older children, others express their maternal gifts in spheres wholly other than the traditional, domestic one. But it was in attempting to analyze my desire to care for my small children, and to place that desire in the broader context of women's aspirations and our social life, that it occurred to me that the radical promise of exploring maternal pleasure had remained unfulfilled.

De Beauvoir asked, all those years ago, "What is a woman?," and her answer reverberated in every subsequent treatment of motherhood. "One is not born, but rather becomes a woman," she wrote, meaning that the defining property of the social category "woman" was not her female physique, but her status as "a person who is not expected to set her own agenda in the world."[3] Ever since, it has been hard to rescue our willingness to take care of others from the taint of inauthenticity, to see it as anything other than a refusal of risk or freedom. It has been hard, in other words, to see our desire and choice to care for children as one way we set our own agenda in the world.

It may once have been true that the price of a woman's social acceptance was that she leave her ambitious, striving self outside the door. But today, she is as likely to be urged to leave outside, or at least politely hide, her intensely emotional concern about caring for her children.

The early years of our children's lives give us a unique opportunity to embrace living fully, in all its fatigue, moodiness, laughter, inconvenience, pleasure, and mess. There is a huge list of reasons why such equanimity is hard to attain, from shifts in roles to conflicts between work and family to the pervasive pressures of a materialistic culture to the fear of death. But it is worth asking ourselves: what can we do to help ourselves claim the joy?

A first step that any of us can take is to sit with the problem, whatever form it takes in our lives. We need to listen to the stirrings of our own soul, take responsibility for all our different feelings, and work toward greater discernment of our desire amid the clamor of voices. How do we do that? First, we notice. We notice the clench in our stomach or the low-level spaciness we feel when we leave our baby for the day. We ask ourselves what we can learn from it. We notice our sense of relief when we get out the door and leave our screaming toddler. We turn that sense of freedom over in our minds, trying to learn all we can about its sources. We notice our thought that we are doing "nothing" caring for a baby all day, or the way thoughts about what we need to get done tumble forward when we sit down to read our child a story. We notice what the pressure of too little time feels like, the way it scatters our attention, wears away at our sense of effectiveness, prompts us to try to move the discomfort outside ourselves by looking for someone or something to blame. Noticing does not make bad feelings go away, but it creates slightly more breathing space for our intimate experience, giving us a moment of honest specificity amid the self-persecuting half-truths that usually clog our minds. It can make us more compassionate toward ourselves, and less lonely.

We try to notice things about our children too. We try to decipher their signs and signals from a centered place, neither reading too much into their ups and downs nor denying their significance. We try to notice what they are asking from us, and how they are asking. We try to figure out whether the way they ask (whining, demandingness, tantrums) is making it hard for us to give them what they want or need. A child played on a beach during vacation. He had been there with a nanny for several hours. His mother arrived, and the child soon fell to whining. Minutes later, exasperated, the mother presented him with an ultimatum: "Stop whining, or I'm leaving." It was a heartbreaking scene to witness because it was clear the child was whining because he wanted his mother's attention. Unable or unwilling to receive what he was trying to tell her, the mother turned his (irritating) behavior against him. They missed each other by a mile. Sometimes our children ask for things we can't give, like more of our time. But again, there is value in being aware of their feelings and our own, and in letting our children know we understand their feelings rather than denying them out of anxiety or sadness.

We also try to notice the larger stories we tell ourselves about our lives, the values our choices express. Economic need is obviously a driving force behind mothers' and fathers' employment and the time they spend away from their children. Money is a necessity; it pays for food and shelter, it can make the difference between the life we grew up with and a better life for our children. Money also buys advantages, from safe neighborhoods to SAT prep courses. And discretionary spending really does make one feel better. It meant a lot to me when I could get rid of that Naugahyde recliner and decorate my baby's room. A woman in Juliet Schor's *The Overspent American* was willing to simplify her life in many ways, but she refused to give up her hair-coloring appointments.[4] Such seemingly superficial uses of money can confer an almost primal sense of pride and satisfaction.

At the same time, it is useful to recognize the social and psychological factors that influence the perception of economic need. We need to notice the scaffolding of assumptions that sanction our choices—assumptions about what is necessary to our happiness, what we can't do without, what is central to our membership in a social group—and make sure that they are assumptions we wish consciously and intentionally to endorse. We need to look closely at our situation to discern what constitutes a real constraint and what constraints are not as rigid as they seem.

All of us, from the affluent couple on their third remodel to the working-class couple at Costco, lugging home their wide-screen TV, are so thoroughly influenced by consumerism that it is hard to separate what we need from what we've been conditioned to desire. But it is still worth trying to distance ourselves from our usual assumptions, to ask ourselves what exactly constitutes a material necessity, and to think about it directly in reference to the question of family time. We can even use the exercise as an opportunity for self-knowledge. Over the years, my pock-marked kitchen floor and my overgrown backyard have both served as objects of spiritual contemplation. Each time they have tormented me with an inchoate sense of failure, each time I have felt like fixing them would be the surest route to fixing myself, I have tried to take a step back and calmly recall that the choice not to spend time making money to improve my surroundings was the same choice that allowed me to spend time with the children.

Finally, it is important to notice when we are "choosing away" from spending time with our children and to ask ourselves what that is about. What are some of the powerful ideas that tip the balance of people's choices away from time with children? I remember that around the time when our children were two, four, and seven years old, there was one day each week, Tuesdays, when the babysitter worked all day, from 8 A.M. till 5 P.M. Every other day of the week, I ended my workday by 2 P.M., or I didn't work at all. I came to notice what I called "the Tuesday effect." At around 5:30 or 6 P.M. on Tuesdays, I would frequently have the thought "Oh boy, it's exhausting to be with these kids all day!," only then to realize that I was having this thought *only* on the day when I *wasn't* with them for much of the day. I came to wonder about that.

I knew that at other points in my work life, I had managed to strike an energizing balance between work and caring for children. I would work for a certain number of hours, feel effective and refreshed, and then come home and feel brightened and alert playing with my child. Each activity served to feed the other. And I have read of other women who feel their workday releases them to enjoy their children in the evening. But what I was noticing with the Tuesday effect was more akin to what Arlie Hochschild described in her book *The Time Bind.* She found it was not a simple matter of "lack of time" that deprived children of their parents, but rather that people were "choosing against" time with family by putting in more time at work. Their sense of meaning and effectiveness gradually clustered more and more in their work identity, and home became less and less rewarding. They felt less effective at home; the emotional needs were more unruly, less easily dispatched.[5] Similarly for me, the more I worked on a given day, the more my center of gravity was in my work and the less I could find exactly what there was to enjoy in taking care of my children.

We can use these feelings as a pretext to insist that work simply *is* more interesting, child care simply *is* more boring. Or we can take it as an opportunity to explore what is getting in the way of fully participating in our own family life. Do we have problems with our spouse that we are not confronting? Does the sheer pace at work make the more meandering tempo of childhood seem unbearably slow? Are we so tied to a narrow notion of achievement that time with children seems unproductive? Do we feel vaguely bad about ourselves for our detachment or ineffectualness at home, a feeling we are only able to banish while at work?

The hard truth is that our ability to appreciate something is affected by the time we devote to it. Whether it is a person or a pursuit, one way we treasure it is through the time we give to it. The more time we spend on a relationship (with a child, with nature, with a piece of music), the more we know and the more we appreciate, and the more facets there are to love.

If we notice ourselves choosing away from spending time nurturing our children, each of us needs to ask, Have I set up my life so as to rationalize shying away from any activity, any spiritual practice, that would put me closer to the burning center of my life, to authentic connection? To what extent are my activities oriented toward maintaining my sense of control, or managing my fear of want and insecurity, or stoking my vanity, in a way that is leading me away from experiencing the depth of love I could? The theologian Thomas Merton wrote: "Love affects more than our thinking and our behavior toward those we love. It transforms our entire life. Genuine love is a personal revolution. Love takes your ideas, your desires, and your actions and welds them together in one experience and one living reality which is a new *you*."[6] This is how people talk about becoming parents. This is how women talk about becoming mothers. This is the explosion in one's heart as old as time.

I ride bikes with my children to school in the morning, the oldest on a two-wheeler, the middle one on training wheels, and the youngest in a cart attached to the back of my bike. One day after dropping off the older ones, I climb the hill to the bike path with my solid three-year-old in tow. As I begin mentally carving up my day, wondering how I will fit in my errands, my work, I am suddenly returned to myself by the beauty of the morning—the mist, our chatting, the pumping of my heart. Every time he asks me a question, it makes a difference how I answer it, not so much by the facts I offer but in the way I attend, in the way I keep faith with his earnest effort to make sense of the world. His thirst for knowledge and my power to slake it move me. It lets me notice once again what our time together means for us both. It feels good and right to hallow this morning, this hour. The liberation of the heart which is love, I think, as we whizz along the bike path and count our friends the ducks.

NOTES

1. Giuseppe Tomasi di Lampedusa, *The Leopard* (New York: Pantheon, 1991), 277–78.

2. "Nostalgia for the present" is a phrase recollected from a commentary on the Chinese philosopher Chuang-Tze, the source of which I was unable to locate. The 1 Corinthians 13:12 quotation is from the King James version of the Bible.

3. Simone de Beauvoir, *The Second Sex*, translated by H. M. Parshley (New York: Vintage Books, 1974), 301; and Nancy Bauer, *Simone de Beauvoir, Philosophy and Feminism* (New York: Columbia University Press, 2001), 171.

4. Juliet B. Schor, *The Overspent American: Upscaling, Downshifting, and the New Consumer* (New York: Basic Book, 1998), 128.

5. See Arlie Russell Hochschild, *Time Bind: When Work Becomes Home and Home Becomes Work* (New York: Metropolitan Books, 1997), chap. 4.

6. Thomas Merton, *Love and Living*, edited by Naomi Burton Stone and Patrick Hart (New York: Farrar, Straus & Giroux, 1979), 28. The phrase "the liberation of the heart which is love" is the Buddha's from Sharon Salzberg, *Lovingkindness* (Boston: Shambhala, 1995), 1.

Part Four

~

Finding Balance

Tell Your Secrets

Ariel Gore

In this short selection, Gore encourages us to put down the mask of "Perfect Mom" and openly share our struggles with each other so that we can form a powerful community of support.

~

GET TOGETHER WITH TRUSTWORTHY MOMS, and tell your secrets. Talk. Describe what it's like to live now. Voice your unspoken feelings about motherhood, your children, your loves, your life, agreeing that nothing is unspeakable. That might seem scary at first. Many of us were taught that even impure *thoughts* are sinful. If that is true, we are all hell-bound. Each of us has had, we must admit, every possible kind of thought.

In a writing group I was once in, each participant was asked to write for ten minutes describing an event or thought sequence she considered unspeakable. I thought for a few minutes and focused on the one thing I had never told anyone. And then I proceeded to tell it. I described the afternoon in Italy after I brought my daughter home from the hospital. I was sitting with her in front of a crackling fire when the urge to throw her in it, blanket and all, struck me like a demon out of nowhere. I was not conscious of wanting to hurt her. I was not conscious of much. Perhaps I hoped to make her immortal, like the ancient Greek goddesses.

I was shaking as I read the pages to my writing group. The story was, to me, unspeakable, and the memory of it had haunted me for many months. Later, I included the sequence in a fictional story and, finally, as truth in my first book. No mother I have ever shared the story with has been terribly shocked. My experience, it turned out, was commonplace. Still, when that first book was about to be published, I sat down with my daughter on the end of her bed and told her the story so that she would hear it from me in a loving tone rather than hear it being discussed on some radio show or read it herself in the book. As I told her, I imagined I would have to explain myself, assure her that I would never do such a thing, promise that she has always been loved and wanted. I underestimated her. At age eight she already knew, as Muriel Rukeyser has pointed out, "the universe is made up of stories, not atoms." She responded with a tale of her own and told me of an urge she considered impure and a dream in which she acted on that unspeakable urge.

Some secrets are necessary for survival. But most of the secrets we keep are neither necessary nor helpful. In myth and psychology, it is well understood that that which is unspoken *becomes* unspeakable. It grows out of control like a thick-rooted weed that can strangle every perfectly placed plant and flower in a garden.

In consciousness-raising groups of the early 1970s, women gathered and—over tea or wine—told the truth about their lives. The result, of course, was that the world split open. The movement that emerged from those consciousness-raising groups revolutionized virtually every facet of American culture. Mothers have been slow to follow suit. Our perfect-mother myths persist. Silences and taboos around maternal ambivalence, maternal rage, and even maternal mad love endure. The roots of those taboos are thick and deep. It is time to pull them up.

I'll never get used to the reality that motherhood is such an isolating experience. There's hardly a more common profession, yet many of us feel completely alone. Our individual homes and our time constraints keep us from one another. And labels—bad mother, good mother, stay-at-home mother, working mother, single mother, and the rest—not only encourage guilt and undermine our efforts but also divide us as potential allies.

Women approach me, call me, and e-mail me asking for advice on various aspects of mothering, but often isolation is their real ache. Simply listening is the most profound help we can offer each other.

We may consider the choices we have to make for our families to be some of the most daunting and far-reaching decisions we will make in our lifetimes. Because of that, and because of the mother-guilt our culture hands us, we often grow defensive about our choices. But as we learn to stop judging ourselves, we can also practice not judging other mamas. In our years of parenting, we will want to connect with moms who share our child-rearing philosophies. But if we are also open to other possibilities, if we can learn to simply listen, we can begin to remedy the isolation of motherhood. We can see each other through.

On hipmama.com, moms share parenting philosophies and sometimes debate what is best for our children. Because the forum is large and diverse, the debates sometimes generate self-righteous or defensive postings. But when a mother posted anonymously at midnight that she was considering suicide, that she'd sent her children to stay with her mother and had her death plans in place, everyone abandoned their debates and posted healing thoughts. All night, new messages appeared on the board. The original poster was silent, but the other mothers—not knowing whether the woman was still sitting and watching her monitor in the dark—did not give up. By morning I was getting worried phone calls and e-mail messages. Did I know who Anonymous was? Was she still alive? Still online? What could we do now?

Twelve hours later the woman in crisis posted again. She had been there all along, reading the other mothers' posts, thinking, refusing to call a hotline or any of the mothers online who offered their phone numbers, waiting, staying connected to this one forum where she felt comfortable. We knew nothing about this woman's parenting. We knew virtually nothing about her life. But we saw her through. Maybe she is online right now, seeing another mother through.

Simplicity

Katrina Kenison

This selection draws attention to our tendency to overdo it as mothers. Whether it's birthday parties, holiday celebrations, or "enriching activities," things often get excessive. Kenison suggests that more is not better for kids and families, and she offers some practical advice on how to scale back.

~

TWO WEEKS BEFORE EASTER, I visit a friend whose children are the same age as mine. When I arrive, she is just cleaning up after an afternoon of coloring eggs with her son and daughter. There are Ukrainian masterpieces, painstakingly created with special tools, dyes, and wax. In addition, they have made stenciled eggs, brilliant glitter eggs, and marbelized eggs, all from kits ordered from a catalog. Some of the eggs feature paintings of flowers and bunnies. Others have been blown out, colored with vegetable dye, and arranged in a basket filled with real, growing grass, planted in March so that it would reach its peak for Easter weekend.

While the children head outside to play, my friend sweeps glitter off the floor, scrubs the table, and washes tiny paintbrushes. The results of their labors are breathtaking, and I ooh and ahh over every egg. They *are* beautiful. But, she confesses with a sigh, she has done most of them herself. The Ukrainian kit proved too complicated for the kids, and the stencils were difficult to do. The children each made a couple of glitter eggs, but they ended up with glue all over their hands and soon lost interest. "Next year," my friend says, laughing, "we're going back to the basic $2.99 kit from CVS!"

I think of those Easter eggs now as I set out to write about simplicity. So often, it seems, *we* are the ones who make our own lives more complicated than they need to be. We set the bar too high, take on too much, turn small doings into big ones. In part the culture is to blame—as each holiday rolls around, we confront an ever-expanding array of merchandise to go with it. There is more to see, more to do, more to buy, than ever before. And how easy it is to fall into thinking that living well means partaking of all that's offered. With so many options and opportunities to choose from, it can be a challenge just figuring out where to draw the line.

Why settle for food coloring and vinegar when you can create an artistic treasure instead? Why stop at birthday cake and ice cream at home when you can rent an indoor playground and invite the whole class? Why spend the Saturday before Christmas sledding with the family when you could all be attending the annual downtown holiday extravaganza?

Why indeed? The fact is, the marketers of this world have gotten very good at thinking of new ways to create desires for goods and services and experiences that didn't even exist a generation ago. As a result, we end up offering too much to our children and taking on too much ourselves.

It is not enough, anymore, to pull together a Halloween costume from the dress-up bin, add a few extra touches, and head out the door to go trick-or-treating. The store-bought costumes are more elaborate, more expensive, and more grisly every year. There are decorations to buy, light shows to orchestrate on the front lawn, haunted houses to visit, and a week's worth of pre-Halloween activities to attend. Last fall my neighbor's six-year-old daughter had been in and out of her costume so many times that she refused to put it back on for Halloween night. She'd been a ballerina in a parade, at school, and at two parties. The novelty had worn off.

I know a little boy who pitched a tantrum at the end of an elaborate birthday party because his goody bag didn't have enough treats in it. At another, children scrambled on all fours to pick up candy scattered from a piñata and then protested because there wasn't enough. Over the past couple of years, my boys have attended birthdays featuring pony rides, a visit from Batman, wild animals, indoor rock climbing, gymnastics, and an inflated space jump, rented by the hour. I've seen overexcited kids fall apart and more than one exhausted mother weeping in the kitchen.

What message do our own excesses send to our children? In our efforts to create special occasions for them, are we losing sight of what's really important? Are these elaborate productions crowding out the kinds of simple, heartfelt celebrations that truly enrich our lives and delight our children?

A few weeks ago, a well-known storyteller came to our town. I made the plans: Jack and a friend would have an early dinner at our house, and then we would enjoy an evening of stories downtown. We ate at five-thirty, bundled into boots and raincoats, and set out in a downpour. The library meeting room was full of wet, boisterous children, ranging in age from two to thirteen—a tough audience at the best of times. But this was six-thirty, mothers were worn out and bedraggled, and the children were rollicking with energy. I hoped that our storytelling celebrity would dim the fluorescent lights, gather the children into a circle, bring a hush to the crowded room. But, it seemed, the mood was already set, and that was what he played to, unleashing a torrent of voices, antics, and impersonations in an effort to capture the attention of this scattered group.

"How come no one is listening?" whispered Jack.

"I think it's past my bedtime," confided four-year-old Nick.

And I had to ask myself, What on earth are we doing here?

Of course, hindsight is easy. But had I brought a little more thought to our agenda that evening, I would have realized that these two small children did not require an outing in order to experience something special. How much better off we would have been staying home on that stormy night, lighting a fire in the fireplace, and inviting Jack's friend for dinner and a story by firelight in our own living room. Once again I was reminded: If I pause long enough to listen to my own inner voice, rather than heeding some external call to go, see, and do, I make better choices for us all.

It takes conviction to say, "This is enough"—whether it be enough holiday events, enough guests at a party, enough presents, or simply enough activities for next Saturday. And it is hard to feel confidence in our own choices, in our own sense of limits, when everyone around us seems convinced that more and bigger is better.

But I am learning. When I find myself worrying, Can I pull this whole thing off? instead of looking forward to a special day, I know it's because I have allowed an event to become more extravagant and ambitious than it needs to be. There is another way. We don't have to make everything into such a big deal. We can choose simplicity over complication. And what relief there is in simplicity. Here's a start:

~ Downscale holiday celebrations. Keep the focus on family, on meaningful rituals and traditions, and on simple activities. Give fewer gifts, and take more time to enjoy them. One year we bought Christmas presents for a needy family and agreed that we would pay for those gifts by scaling down our own giving to one gift per person. No one felt deprived; in fact, I think we all felt relieved. When I ask my children what they love most about our Christmas, their answers remind me that simple really is best: reading our Christmas books, the advent calendar, our annual carol sing with the family next door, lighting the ting-a-ling on Christmas Eve.

~ Set a limit on holiday activities. (One Easter egg hunt is enough!)

~ Don't feel guilty about skipping events that everyone else attends. Your children need you and your attention, not more activities. Last year we didn't go to the end-of-the-year barbecue and pool party for Henry's second-grade class—simply because we needed a quiet family day more than we needed one more end-of-school event. As I remind my children when the birthday party invitations start to pile up, "You don't have to go to everything." Watching us manage our own lives sensibly, our children will learn to set limits, too.

~ Celebrate birthdays in a way that honors the qualities you love in your child. They don't have to be big productions;

make them expressions of love instead: a special meal, an outing with a friend, a birthday ritual carried on year after year. My sons each have a birthday candle waiting for them on the breakfast table; at dinnertime, each family member offers a birthday wish for the coming year.

~ Whether you're decorating the Christmas tree, making latkes, or coloring Easter eggs, remember that the process is more important for your child than the outcome. Keep the process simple, and your child will enjoy it more.

~ Set limits and stick to them. In our house, no one is allowed to wear their Halloween costumes until Halloween night. Although it's hard for the kids to wait, it's worth it. The anticipation builds, and Halloween lasts for a few hours instead of a whole week. Does anyone really want a week of Halloween?

~ You don't have to prove anything to anybody. Christmas is not a competition, a seder is not a cooking contest, a birthday doesn't need to be a blowout, a dinner party can be potluck.

~ Celebrate small blessings and offbeat occasions. Once we take the pressure off ourselves to do things in a big way, we find more reasons to celebrate life's little moments. My son Jack and I once made a birthday cake for Curious George. Half birthdays are reason enough to enjoy a special meal. Hot summer days suggest impromptu lemonade parties. For children, every day holds potential for celebration and ceremony—the first day of spring, the first snowfall, the harvest moon. A song, a poem read aloud, a ritual, or a special snack—it doesn't take much to create a celebration that affirms life and connects us to the natural order of things: animals, wind, sky, and earth.

Yesterday we colored our own Easter eggs. Taking my friend's experience to heart, I kept it simple. Five bowls of colored water. There was magic enough in that.

In simplicity there is freedom—
freedom to do less and to enjoy more.

I'm Breathing, Are You?

Nancy Hathaway

Nancy Hathaway is a mother of two and a Zen teacher. In this essay, she reflects on how our lived experience as mothers is often so different from what we want or expect. She goes on to share some practical tools from her Zen training that can help any mother to become more fully present, clear, and compassionate amid the daily chaos of parenthood. Hathaway emphasizes how the body—particularly our breath and posture—is a mother's ever-present resource.

~

IT BEGAN AS A QUIET, peaceful day, as mornings with mothers and children at home often begin. But as the day went on, the activity and energy of the household increased. Grandmother came to visit, friends came to play with treasured toys, tiredness came on, and hunger appeared. So, he lost it. Five years old and screaming, a full-blown temper tantrum. Grandmother, (my mother), began getting uncomfortable with his behavior, saying: "If he doesn't stop screaming, I will need to go home." This was the beginning of her three-day visit.

I lead my child into our little at-home meditation room. This room is bare and full of space—loving, attentive, non-judgmental space. It has been furnished over time with breath and posture, with attention and chanting. I sit with him on a pile of bed pillows and hold the flailing, screaming mind for ten minutes, for twenty minutes, for thirty minutes. What a meditation retreat! How long will this mind go on? I hang in, mindful of my breath, posture, and body sensations, mindful of us both. Staying with my breath, I keep an upright posture, and quietly chant *Kwan Seum Bosal* (a Korean Zen chant that invokes love and compassion). Finally, at sixty minutes, the flailing quiets and disappears; the mind of smiles and hugs and cuddles appears. We sit quietly breathing together.

A week later the screaming mind appears again in my five-year-old. This time he takes me by the hand and leads me into the safe space. On this day the screaming mind only needed ten minutes. And the next time only four. And the next time only. . . . Now, at eighteen years old, when this young adult/child who knows me so well sees any tension in my face, he lovingly says, with a relaxed, strong posture, full of confidence, and with a smile, "I'm breathing, are you?"

Parenting is a challenge. Our children cry. Our children throw temper tantrums—in supermarkets, in quiet spaces, in the most embarrassing of places. Our children whine, fight, say sassy things. They push our buttons. They want dinner when we're not ready to make dinner, and they don't want dinner when it is ready. Our children want one more story, just when we are beat, exhausted, and need to do just a few more things before hitting the sack ourselves. Our children look into our eyes and with the sweetest of faces say, "Mommy will you play with me?" while we are in the middle of something, whatever it is, and it's hard to let go of what we're doing or it's not appropriate to let go of what we're doing. Perhaps dinner is burning and the phone is ringing and someone is at the door while at the same time our children want our attention—and they want it RIGHT NOW!

We want the best for our children, our families, ourselves; we want family life to be peaceful and happy. But family life is often uncomfortable and filled with intense feelings. The question is: What do we do with this discomfort? What do we do with our feelings? How do we relate to the strain of wanting something other than this?

Many of us have come to expect family life to look like images from *Martha Stewart Living*. Magazine pictures begin to seem like the norm. If our life doesn't look like that, we think something is wrong. The few of us who do have the Martha Stewart house realize that something is missing. We spend much of our time and energy trying to get it all together. We put a lot of time into our makeup, but our faces have frowns; our clothing is well thought out, but our posture is bent over; our kitchens are big and glamorous, but the warmth of the hearth is missing. We have romanticized the material world, thinking that it brings happiness. We are surrounded by messages from the media that tell us if we have this or that, we will have it all. But what is it all? Do we take the time to ask ourselves what it is that we are *really* looking for?

The simple answer is we're looking for happiness. We have come to believe that happiness will come from stopping the crying child, the temper tantrum, the whining, the sassy talk, the loud music. We try to avoid pain, and we seek comfort—often by acquiring more and more of something, anything—instead of wanting, accepting, appreciating, and receiving what we actually have.

There is another way. As a longtime student of Zen and the mother of two sons, I have found certain Buddhist teachings and practices to be extremely helpful in working with the inherent challenges and discomforts of raising children. In particular, the core Buddhist teachings of the Four Noble Truths and the practice of meditation—in the midst of regular, everyday life—have guided and supported me through the parenting years. These teachings have no religious boundaries, they are remarkably universal— mothers of any background can draw on them for insight and guidance. Meditation and the Four Noble Truths point us in the direction that we all long for as human beings on this planet together: they point us in the direction of freedom from suffering.

THE FOUR NOBLE TRUTHS OF PARENTHOOD

1. Parenthood will always include discomfort and pain.

The first Noble Truth of Buddhism is that life often fails to meet our hopes and expectations. As parents, we face this essential fact when our children cry, lose a favorite toy, feel left out, get sick. When pain arises, more often than not we get tight, we turn off, we resist. We try to push it all away. Many mothers think that if they are "good mothers" their children will not be uncomfortable, will not cry, will not feel angry, will not have any real problems. But the first Noble Truth of Buddhism reminds us that difficulty and pain will always be part of life, whether we are young or old, rich or poor, whether we are the haves or the have nots.

2. Suffering is caused by wanting life to be other than
the way it is.

Suffering arises when we want something other than what we are presented with. And, of course, we often want something other than what we get. Our children are crying, and we want them to be smiling. They are throwing a temper tantrum in the grocery store, and we want them to be cute and make it easy for us to do our shopping. Our child wets the bed or the house is a mess, and we yell out of frustration.

The way we usually try to find happiness—by controlling or forcing the situation to be the way we want it to be—is, in fact, the route to more suffering. Of course we want peaceful situations, happy children, a clean house. But if this is not the reality, how do we deal with it? How do we relate to the inherent challenges, frustrations, and pain of daily life with children? So often we create more unnecessary suffering by insisting that our children be different from who they are, that this moment be different than it is. We create more suffering when we try to ignore the pain, the discomfort, or when we get angry at it. In short, whenever we try to get rid of what *is,* we get into trouble.

3. *Freedom from suffering is possible.*

The third Noble Truth is fairly simple. Since we know the cause of suffering (wanting things to be other than they are), we can find a solution. There is a way out of this trap. Then we ask, What is this way out of suffering? How can we create true happiness instead of being led down the old, worn path of creating more suffering?

4. *The way out of suffering is learning to be with life as it is and making that our practice.*

More traditionally, the fourth Noble Truth of Buddhism outlines a specific way out of suffering known as the Eightfold Path (right view, right thought, right speech, right action, right livelihood, right effort, right mindfulness, right meditation). In broad terms, the Eightfold Path consists of powerful daily practices for learning to live in harmony with life as it is, rather than constantly trying to force life into being what we want it to be. Parenthood provides countless opportunities to do just that—to drop our expectations, our hopes, our preconceptions, and to learn to be with life just as it is, in *this* moment.

The first step is to become fully aware of what *is*. For example, I am in the supermarket and my child is crying. Embarrassment arises within me, the look of the woman next to me suggests to me that I am committing a mortal sin by having a screaming child. I feel tightness in my chest. I hear the voice in my head that says my child shouldn't be screaming!

This is my experience, this is the pain of *this* moment. I breathe and take a moment to notice my thoughts, feelings, physical sensations. I let them in. This is what *is*. You might ask how I can do this in the middle of such a situation, feeling harassed and under pressure. It takes practice and courage and faith. The more we do it, the more we open to the fullness of the moment, the more we know in our mind and body that it works. It doesn't take long before the situation starts to shift. We begin to feel a little space and coolness arises. Then from a calmer, more balanced place, where we are aware of what is and accept what is, we find that we know what to do. We know how to set limits for our child or we know that we must let go of our own expectations. We act with greater compassion and wisdom for all.

Too often, when the going gets tough with our children, we try to escape our reality. We lose our courage to live in the moment. When our feelings start to intensify, we try to run away from them by blaming the situation on someone else, usually someone closest to us like our spouse or our children. As strange as it sounds, if we open to discomfort and experience it one hundred percent, then we experience freedom, liberation, true love.

By opening to the moment, we are able to slow down and breathe into the middle of our discomfort. We are able to be with our children, see their discomfort fully, see their pleasure fully, smell the flowers, really see the smiles on their faces. We notice the I-want-a-perfect-child dream, the I-want-a-bigger-house dream, the I-want-you-to-be-other-than-you-are dream. By noticing the dream, we acknowledge it; by acknowledging it, we sometimes don't have to act on it. The essential point is that the way out of suffering is to practice accepting what *is*—accepting the whole realm, accepting discomfort, ours, theirs—accepting it all.

PUTTING THE TEACHINGS INTO PRACTICE

As mothers, how do we use the Four Noble Truths to help us to become more present with our children? How do we start to live in the real moment right here, right now, rather than in the dream, whatever dream it is? The idea of living in the moment is simple, but attaining it is not so easy. Old habits die hard—old patterned ways of being, of doing things, of living life. To change these old habits, we need to practice. We need to practice making a choice that is not based on feelings of fight-or-flight, not trying to change what *is*, not trying to control the situation, but rather by choosing to live *with* discomfort. So how do you actually do this in the real world, in daily life? How do you turn this vision of wakeful parenting into a reality? In Zen, we begin with the body.

Posture

In Zen, proper meditation posture is the basis of enlightenment—some say it's all you need. What is proper posture for the practice of parenthood? It is to stand erect in the middle of life, with dignity, grace, and an open heart. The practice is to do this at the kitchen sink, behind the wheel of the car, pushing the grocery cart, changing diapers. The other choice is to stand rounded over, chest hollowed in as we sink in and try to cover or hide our pain, oftentimes subconsciously. If we stand straight, or sit upright, with shoulders back, chest and heart open, head upright, we automatically become more aware and awake.

In traditional Zen meditation, proper posture also includes how we hold our faces. Zen practitioners are sometimes instructed to do sitting meditation with a slight smile on their faces. Not a fake, wide smile, but a gentle, half-smile. A simple practice for mothers is to bring this kind of smile into the daily life of parenting.

Many of us have always wanted to be a mother. We knew that this would involve making dinner for our families, changing diapers, getting up early, and so on, and yet here we are making dinner and wishing that we were somewhere else, "Oh, the sunny, warm Caribbean . . ." Yet this same exact experience, including the Caribbean dream, can change from an expression of our suffering into a moment of true happiness if we put a small smile on our faces. It is that simple. The same exact scenario of wanting to escape from our lives can bring us happiness if we are fully present to it, aware of the longing, aware of exactly what this present moment brings. Doing so, we become less attached and have more distance, seeing this scenario as manifesting on its own. The practice of the half smile takes the ego out of the situation, adds some space, brings gentle awareness of what *is*. Try it. Change a messy diaper mumbling, grumbling, complaining—then add a smile, being aware of it all. This small, relaxed smile can make a surprisingly big difference.

Breath

The next helpful step in becoming a more wakeful and compassionate parent is being with the breath, especially when the going gets tough. Feel the breath as it comes in, as it goes out. Follow the breath with your attention. The breath is always with you. Notice how the in-breath has a beginning, middle, and end to it. Then the out-breath has a beginning, middle, and end, going out and out until it stops. Notice the small pause between the out-breath and the in-breath. The breath is always with us, the gift of life.

Breathing within the chaos of parenting brings us balance and perspective, and it reconnects us with our loving nature. As a parent, conscious breathing was not so easy for me within the hectic pace of daily life. When I just couldn't give my breath attention, I would use a word that would help me to be in the present moment. Any word is fine. I would often use the name of the bodhisattva of compassion, Kwan Seum Bosal (also known as the goddess Kwan Yin). Repeating a special word over and over again can be very powerful and enjoyable. It cuts down on thinking, which helps us to live in the moment. Our excess mental energy quiets, and we open more to our children, to what is at hand, in a gentler, more peaceful and relaxed way. Try it, you might like it. You can use any word: "one," "peace," "now," "here," or as my Zen teacher would say, even "Coca Cola" is okay. It's not the word itself but what the saying of the word does to quiet the racing mind.

The Bell of Attention

Ringing a bell in the home is a wonderful way to remind ourselves to breathe, straighten our posture, and come back to the present moment. Find a bell that is attractive and easy to ring. Create a special table that invites attention, presence, and respect as the setting for the bell. This table could include seasonal flowers or objects that your children might collect, such as horse chestnuts or acorns. This should not be a place of forgetfulness, but a place that is alive with change. You could add a frame to display school papers for a few days at a time. Place the bell on the table so that it invites people to ring it.

Anyone in the family, child or adult, may ring the bell at any time. When the bell is rung, everyone stops what they are doing and takes three conscious breaths (and perhaps the parents remember to smile). This bell can give children a wonderful sense of power. They can do something that makes everyone stop—for a positive reason. Children are sensitive, more so than we realize. When they need attention they can ring this bell and sometimes their need will be satisfied by taking three breaths . . . sometimes.

My Zen teacher taught me to continually come back to my breath, straighten my posture, and ask myself, "Right now, what is *this*?" This simple, skillful technique is always within our reach. When someone rings this bell, it will be a reminder for all to return to, "Right now, what is *this*?" The bell also reminds us that the direction of our home is to inhabit the present moment, because the present moment is the only place where we can deeply connect with our children and find real happiness.

Knowing that this is your direction, your children may start to notice when you are stressed and may know that if you raise your voice, it's because you've temporarily lost your openness, not because they are bad. They may also see when they are not acting compassionately and may develop a skill for coping with their own stressful situations—breathing before an exam, straightening their posture as they get up in front of the class while giving a report, taking a quiet moment before a foul shot in front of the whole school.

As mothers, we must make a conscious choice about how we want to live. The swirl of the society is rushing around us. Do we want to live in a dream, or do we want to experience reality? As we experience what it really means to be a mother, we begin to connect to all mothers, for we all want to end suffering and find true happiness for ourselves, for our children, and for all beings. I call this realizing "mother's mind."

As we learn through our experience what it means to be a loving, compassionate mother, we encounter each situation as our child. Using the resources of the present moment, we become fulfilled and truly happy even as we face our biggest challenges because we know that this, too, is part of being a mother in this universe. As we practice on this path of awareness, we expand our love to include more and more of the pleasures and pains of what it means to be human. This is the way things are as a parent.

Motherhood is the perfect path for spiritual practice, for enlightenment. It puts us right in the guts of this life: we love our children to death, we want the very best for them. We do so much for them, making great efforts to get them what we think they need. But what our children really need is for their mothers to be present with them. You can give them the tiniest of birthday cakes, the smallest of presents, and if it is done with real attention and wakefulness, what could be better?

And when they cry, over the loss of a toy or the loss of a friend, what is it that they really want? Yes, they want this particular thing, this or that, but on a basic level they want their mothers to be present with them while they cry. They want a mother who can stand in the middle of chaos and breathe, and have a slight smile on her face, because chaos is the way it is. So please be present in it, and give them what they—and you—really want.

Good-bye Herd

Muffy Mead-Ferro

When I was pregnant with my first child, I asked a friend who had two children what equipment I would need to buy for the new baby. Our phone conversation generated a page-long list of expensive "must have" items. By contrast, a friend's sixty-something mother told me that all you really need for a new baby is a drawer and a sink. In this selection, Muffy Mead-Ferro, a self-described "slacker mom," questions the excessive consumerism of new motherhood and praises the lost art of "making do."

~

FOR US MOMS OR MOMS-TO-BE in these information-awash and overachieving times, it feels as though, somehow, we've become everyone else's property. Wards of the state. Imbeciles.

We can't put a toe out of bed in the morning without feeling the pressure to buy a bunch of expensive equipment and do a whole load of nutty and, frankly, inconvenient things in the interest of being a supermom and producing a superkid. We're inundated with instructions on how best to achieve these goals. And we're not supposed to question either one—the instructions or the goals.

It makes me want to put my toe right back under the covers and keep it there.

About halfway through my pregnancy with my daughter Belle, I began to balk. By then I was well acquainted with the graphic testimonials and detailed advice that this physical state invariably elicits from people. But I started to take exception to all the guidance I was getting.

An early indication that I might end up a slacker mom was a tendency toward sarcasm. "Like I need a smart baby," I muttered, when hearing about the latest device for stimulating her intellect in-vitro.

This negative attitude was accompanied by recurring fits of laziness. "When pigs fly," I thought, as I evaluated the odds of my carving out time to engage in such dreary activities as charting her fluid intake and bowel movements.

These disquieting and politically incorrect feelings increased in frequency and intensity throughout my pregnancy. Yes, kind of like labor pains. I did my best to ignore them, however. I hadn't really started to see myself as a slacker, much less feel good about the idea.

Just the opposite, in fact. While spending 60 hours a week in a love-hate relationship with the largest client at the advertising agency where I worked, I was dutifully taking all my prenatal vitamins. I'd quit smoking crack altogether. Actually, I never smoked crack, but I was made to feel that dry martinis and double lattes amounted to the same thing, so I quit drinking both of them.

I was also reading all five of my pregnancy-advice books simultaneously. And, I was trying to keep up with all the expert guidance I was getting from magazines, TV shows, websites and complete strangers standing next to me in the department store aisle. I was pregnant—the chips were down.

I was never even sure what that phrase refers to, but to me it conveyed the paranoia I felt. "The chips are down," I kept reminding myself.

In other words, do not screw up now, because there's no turning back.

But I was already feeling inadequate. For instance, I could not find the time to sit around with headphones stretched over my abdomen playing Mozart to my fetus in an effort to make her better at her multiplication tables.

I had seen the tummy-headphone outfits in catalogs, along with the proof of their effectiveness. Well, not proof, exactly, but lots of glowing testimonials from non-slacker moms whose objectivity was somehow never in doubt. I didn't buy them though, and my task-oriented personality was making me feel guilty.

From what the product description promised, these contraptions stood at least some chance of turning my kid into a real egghead. So how could I justify not buying them? How could I let day after irreplaceable day of my pregnancy go by as my fetus, the little slacker, just loafed the time away in my dull, unstimulating womb?

They're expensive? I'm busy? Feeble excuses, considering what was apparently at stake.

But it was all I could do just to hold down a job, keep appointments with my hair stylist, and try and get the nursery put together. Those last two weren't easy, either. My responsibilities to my clients involved weekly travel. I didn't have a lot of time at home, much less in baby supply stores.

I did eventually set aside a Saturday for a marathon baby-apparatus shopping spree with the help of a super-organized girlfriend. She'd had her first baby eight months before, so from my standpoint she knew just scads about child-rearing. Looking back,

I realize (as I'm sure she does) that she was as addled as I was. A victim of all the same marketing campaigns and societal pressure that every other new mom is subjected to.

That day, I was right there with her. She'd generously prepared a four-page list of mission-critical items for me to purchase in a mad race from one end of the city to another. I didn't even question it. I was in that to-hell-with-the-budget frame of mind that it's so easy to get into when you're deranged. Or eight months pregnant.

I spent the entire day, contributing more than my share to the national epidemic of credit card debt. But I only knocked 90 percent of the items off my list, and it was that last tenth that was, illogically, making me feel I was further behind every minute.

In particular, I had yet to receive the bassinet I'd ordered weeks and weeks before from one of the more snooty baby stores, and really didn't know what I would do if that bassinet did not arrive before D-day. My baby needed a place to sleep, for God's sake! I didn't know whether to call the store and continue to hassle them, or just sneak over there with a can of gas and torch the place.

I was a ticking time bomb, basically. Above the neck as well as below.

Thankfully, the evening after that exhausting and expensive day of shopping, I happened to get a phone call from a friend in Alaska. Mother of two, with a third on the way. She had called to check on how my late-in-life pregnancy was going, and to inquire about my career plans following the birth of my baby.

When she asked if I was ready to have this new little person in my life, I was too fixated on the slapdash condition of my nursery to know that she was probably talking about my emotional readiness, not my equipment list. So I told her that I was not even close to being ready because I still required a number of crucial items. Namely, the bassinet.

Her response to this desperate state of affairs was to loudly guffaw. "Are you kidding?" she said. "My little boy slept in a crab crate his first six months."

That silenced me for a speck. I knew I'd heard her right. She said "crab crate." One of those cage-type deals made of nailed-together wooden slats that's been underwater, with crabs in it. Eww. I did feel sorry for the little boy.

That waste of sympathy came and went pretty quickly however. Her little boy didn't care. If he didn't care, why should she? And apparently she wasn't concerned about what other people thought either. That was the most startling and impressive of all. If a mom could get away with this in Alaska . . . right away I saw where this could lead me.

When I got off the phone, I went into the bathroom, looked at the stressed-out woman in the mirror and asked her pointblank, "Are you daft?"

I didn't even recognize myself. I'd grown up on a cattle ranch, for cripes sake. In our family, we were supposed to tell the cows where to go, not join the herd! And I didn't need someone in Alaska telling me how to rough it—I was the daughter of Mary Mead—a woman who stuck us in a mud puddle to play when my brothers and I were little.

My mom did things her own way. She never had a bassinet and she probably never did any of the things I had on my To-Do list. Maybe I wasn't ready to throw that list in the garbage. But I was ready to take a good, hard look at it.

By then I'd changed my mind about the overdue bassinet. In fact, I probably would have called and canceled my order if I hadn't already indicated to the store manager that it was a matter of life and death. There were lots of other places my baby could sleep. A cardboard box was a suite at the Plaza for all she'd know.

I thought as well about the other nursery provisions I'd spent so much money on that day, and I regarded them with a new skepticism. Looking at them objectively for a change, there were a few of them I could still categorize as essentials (thermometer), but more of them would now have to be classified as luxuries (changing table). And to be completely honest with myself, quite a few of them would best be described as a big pile of plastic debris (infant activity center).

I also considered the strains of Mozart's Piano Concerto No. 21 which I wasn't piping into my womb. "My mom never did that," I said to myself, "and I was always pretty good at math." When it occurred to me that Einstein's mom didn't do it either, I went right ahead and crossed that off my list of things to feel guilty about.

My enlightenment never did lead to my newborn sleeping in a cardboard box, though, because the European bassinet I'd been so concerned with arrived in time. At least it was attractive—it wasn't made of yellow plastic. I put it in the same category as Prada loafers, an extravagant personal indulgence. This made me feel a little better about its price tag.

I have no problem with extravagant personal indulgences, by the way. I just want to call them by their real name. And be clear about whether I'm indulging myself or my kid.

The bassinet was a case of me indulging me. It did serve a purpose, too, for about three months. But not an essential purpose. And by then I knew that if anything here was essential, it was that I start thinking for myself.

Of course, thinking for yourself is not exactly easy when you're in that state of pre-baby delivery that seems to dictate an all-out spending binge, decorating rampage, and whirlwind of dusting and vacuuming, right up until your water breaks. I guess this condition goes by the rather congenial term of "nest-building." But, in cases like mine, the term "prenatal lunacy" was probably more apt.

Some of that must be unavoidable, especially if it's your first baby. But I've discovered that being creative and improvising not only saves me a lot of time and money, it's also setting an example that might actually be useful to my children.

The example of making-do.

If you don't know what I mean by "making-do," just ask your grandmother, if you're lucky enough to still have one. Making-do is a way of accomplishing amazing things such as baking up an apple pie with no apples.

My grandmother married into a Wyoming cattle ranching family, and if she didn't know how to make-do before then, she must've learned right away. She tells how it was to raise her little boy and girl (my uncle and my mom) on the ranch in the '30s and '40s. They could only make the five-mile trip into town two or three times during the long, deep winters. And when they did go, it was on a sleigh wagon pulled by two draft horses. Not a quick trip.

Even if she'd lived in town, the local market wouldn't have stocked powdered formula, disposable diapers, prepared baby food, or any of the other things I took for granted, and probably couldn't have gotten along without. They didn't even have apples ten months of the year.

"How did you do it?" I've asked her several times.

"I just did," she always says.

"But how?" I persist. She had none of the proper equipment or instructions by today's standards. But she never describes motherhood as a hardship.

My grandmother wouldn't look down on contemporary moms, though. She would say it's just practical to take advantage of modern conveniences if you've got access to them. But it illustrates the relative nature of "need" when you consider that previous generations have raised lots of happy and healthy babies—even smart ones—without any of the things I had on my baby shopping list.

Listening to my grandmother's recollections has given me a stark perspective on what is—and what is not—an essential baby supply. I thought of her when I opened a baby shower gift that turned out to be one of those gadgets known as wipe-warmers. I'm talking about a little plug-in container that keeps wipes warm, so baby's bottom doesn't feel any change in temperature during a diaper change, for those of you who live in outer Mongolia and don't already know this.

My grandmother still remembers getting her homemade, hand-washed cloth diapers off the clothesline in the cold Wyoming winter.

"It was like bringing in a stack of boards," she says.

Not that they went from there to the baby's bottom. They became warm and pliable enough after hanging all day over a line strung behind the wood stove in her living room.

My mom was also a making-do virtuoso. I suppose she learned that from her mother. Or maybe life on a remote Wyoming cattle ranch dictates that. So might life in a fishing village or a garment district or a mining town. I'm sure most moms of a generation back were better at making-do than we are today. So my family's not unique in that respect.

One way we differed from most American families, though, is that we didn't have television. We tried like mad to get it, and experimented with many dubious reception methods involving tinfoil. But we never could get TV until cable came along, and they finally ran one out to the ranch. By then I was in my teens.

Thanks to that technology gap, I missed out on a huge body of cultural knowledge in which all my friends are conversant. They can all sing the Brady Bunch theme song and the Oscar Meyer jingle. I doubt you were spared those influences the way I was. So you already know what it took me 20 years working in advertising to fully appreciate.

You know that if you've got television, you've got somebody incessantly telling you, over and over, without reprieve (Yes, I'm being redundant—just emphasizing one of the most important ways we all know marketing works.) that you've got to have a certain brand of, say, diapers. It's hard not to be convinced when they show you the droves of babies who've achieved total satisfaction from these diapers. Even if you realize deep down that these babies are, in fact, professional actors.

Even more cunning is when the commercials dramatize your deepest fears in a scenario where the bungling incompetence of the mom is revealed to the world as her baby shows up in a competing brand of diaper, leaking on the mother-in-law's blouse.

By this time, you know on a subconscious level, at least, that you must either be mentally deficient or grossly negligent if you choose not to purchase their product.

Why do advertisers think this kind of guilt-driven message will work with moms? I don't see them speaking this way to fathers, I really don't. Are we mothers that insecure? Is that how we get talked into such harebrained things as abdomen-phones?

I don't know. But I do know what will happen if I buy into all those marketing messages and actually purchase all the kid gear I see touted in parenting magazines or attractively displayed in stores. The first thing that will happen is I'll be bankrupt. But the second thing is I'll be depriving my children of that invaluable life-lesson, taught by example, of making-do.

My mom learned it from my grandmother and I want my kids to learn it from me. Maybe that way, when they grow up, they'll be more resourceful. Which might even get them further ahead than being super-smart.

Whenever I feel like I'm getting caught up in the modern neurosis that seems to accompany child-rearing, I just ask myself, what if I'd had my babies in an isolated Alaskan fishing village and didn't have access to the breast-feeding counselors or toddler-fitness classes? Or what if I were raising my children back on the ranch during the Depression and simply couldn't afford all the educational toys and extracurricular activity fees? Would it mean that my kids were automatically disadvantaged, wouldn't have skills, and wouldn't achieve success in life?

The answer's always "No, no, and no." In fact, I'm more and more convinced that our kids may be quite a bit better off when they don't have all the so-called advantages.

Time-Out for Parents

Cheri Huber and Melinda Guyol

This selection offers a simple meditation practice to help parents under-stand their own needs and access their compassion for themselves and their children. The authors, two Zen teachers, underscore the idea that until we get in touch with ourselves, we can't be fully present and loving to our children. Most writing about "good parenting" gets idealistic and unrealistic. The case study in this excerpt shows us how to put theory into practice amid the mess of real life.

~

*A*s ZEN MEDITATION TEACHERS, we teach people to sit in silence, facing a blank wall. The idea is to learn to slow down, to become quiet in mind and body, subtle in attention. This prac-tice can enable us to experience who we really are, our True Nature, our essence, God. Variations of this practice are found in all major religions throughout history.

In the system of controlling children's behavior called "time-out," angry or misbehaving children are isolated, made to be quiet, and sometimes even required to sit facing a wall. This method has been in vogue long enough that we are now receiving students who, when asked to sit quietly by themselves in meditation, feel punished, feel "bad."

We've noticed that much of the discussion and literature on parenting focuses on the parent-child interaction, specifically on how to get the child to behave. It seems to us that a vital aspect of the interaction is then neglected. That aspect is the parent's internal process.

We'd like to change the concept of time-out. Instead of punishing children by sending them into isolation, let's offer ourselves a time-out to discover our own needs, and our own true selves. Then we will have everything *we* need in order to give our children what *they* need. Jan and Alix's story illustrates this point.

Jan and Alix's Story

I had come to dread picking up my five-year-old daughter, Alix, each day. I was tense and drained from work pressures and the long commute, and what greeted me every evening at the daycare center was a cranky, whiny, tired, hungry child. It often seemed that her one purpose in life was to make me more miserable.

I tried saying to Alix the kinds of things I'd heard parents say.

"Stop whining and crying."

"We'll be home in five minutes so stop it now!"

"You're giving me a headache."

Nothing I said improved the situation. The real message I was giving Alix was that her feelings were not okay.

I so dreaded my daughter's whining and crying that I would steel myself and tough it out, or I would threaten her with a time-out. When my words had no effect on her behavior, I would feel out of control and would resort to raising my voice, which made me feel like I had lost it. I felt defeated and inadequate; I felt like a bad parent. Many days I would end up with a headache, shouting at my daughter, with her shouting and crying in response.

I tried explaining to Alix what behavior was not okay, such as whining, shouting at me, and being noncompliant. However, because I was so tired and tense and miserable, I was usually shouting and whining, too! When explaining appropriate behavior didn't work, I sank to having candy waiting in the car, which made me feel guilty and usually ruined Alix's appetite for dinner.

I desperately wanted to end our suffering but could not see how to do that. I had no reserves left to be calm, loving, and compassionate, and I kept looking for solutions outside myself.

If we hope to give children the gift of a happy, responsible, fully alive adulthood, we must first live that way ourselves.

"Yes," you may say, "but I can't take time for me. The children's needs have to come first."

To this widely held belief, we offer this observation, gleaned from countless airplane trips: A flight attendant's voice is heard on the pre-flight safety video as oxygen masks are shown dropping from overhead compartments, "For those traveling with small children, be sure to put your oxygen mask on first before assisting your child."

The message is clear. If you aren't alive, you can't keep your child alive. A parent whose needs aren't being met has few resources to offer a child. And to be alive requires that we pay attention to ourselves in a new way.

Take a moment just to be with yourself. Turn your attention to your breathing. Take a few slow, deep breaths and notice what it's like to be present with the thoughts, emotions, and sensations you are experiencing. As you breathe, allow your attention to move into your body with your breath. Is your body tense? Relaxed?

Ask yourself, "What am I feeling?" Notice how you find the answer to that question. Where do you look to find your feelings?

Notice your thoughts. What are they saying? Are you aware that different parts of you say different things?

Simply be present in this moment, just noticing.

Most of us can access the kind, loving, compassionate parent fairly easily when things are going well, when we check on the child who's sleeping like a little angel, or when the child has done something particularly sweet or loving or adorable. At these times, we're aware that we love this child unconditionally and we feel great tenderness and warmth and affection.

We lose sight of that unconditional love when we leave the place of the kind parent, and identify with a part of us who is tired, stressed, hungry, and perhaps emotionally very young. If we stop for a moment, we can realize when this is happening to us.

The kind, loving parent speaks a very different language from the person who is stressed and overwhelmed. Everything about those two people is different: one is relaxed, comfortable, open, loving; the other is tight, tense, worried, nervous, short-tempered. When we recognize we're being that overwhelmed, tired person, or when we realize we've slipped into a very young, petulant, punishing, blaming part of ourselves, we can stop, take a deep breath, and step back to see ourselves from a broader perspective.

From this clearer place, it can be a powerful experience to take a few long, deep breaths and recall a time when our child was being particularly loving, a time when our child needed us and we were there. We can remember when we looked forward to being a parent, when we wanted to have a child to raise and care for, and doing so, we can feel our hearts open.

In that moment of stepping back and taking a breath, we can stop believing the story we are telling ourselves about how awful the situation is, how intolerable, how it shouldn't be this way, how we can't stand it. In those few breaths we can call forth the kind, parental part of ourselves and change the nature of the interaction. We change it for our child and we change it for ourselves. We both receive the kindness and love.

Another way to find the compassionate parent in ourselves is to bring up an image of how we look when we're yelling at our child. Just step back and see how we (imagine) we look. How is that person feeling? What does that person need? By seeing ourselves as if we were someone else, we can often find a more caring perspective.

We want to practice regularly evoking the compassionate parent, not just in stressful situations. If we practice in ordinary situations, finding compassion when we are stressed won't be so hard. We'll have experience doing it.

As we're taking time out, we want to identify consciously with the loving part of ourselves. We want to remind ourselves that this is how we want to be with our child, this is the choice we want to make. We practice going to this place so that, when we are in a stressful situation, the compassionate parent is close by.

Simply put, we're learning to be for ourselves the parent we want to be for our child. When we are that parent, we feel taken care of, the child feels taken care of, our partner feels taken care of, everyone feels taken care of. Finding our way back to an unconditionally loving relationship with ourselves gives us access to the kind, compassionate, loving presence we want for our child.

It's simple. When we are living in conscious, compassionate awareness, we provide what we need for ourselves, and we provide to our children what they need. We are modeling the adulthood we want for our children, which we hope they will model for their children.

Jan and Alix's Story, Continued

It never occurred to me to look inward, to see what needs of mine were not being met. I did not realize how tired and drained I was—that I actually had nothing left for Alix. I took her behavior as a personal attack, and the interaction between us degenerated into a power struggle.

Plan a few minutes each day as your exclusive time-out. Treat this time as a gift to yourself, rather than as another "should" to burden your life. It's important to have quiet, alone time to create the inner peace we long to experience. Daily life, particularly for parents, is so filled with demands, distractions, and urgent, must-do activities, that the opportunity for this kind of time-out gets lost in the shuffle. Taking a daily time-out might be the most important thing you ever do.

When we take time-out for ourselves, even for only a few minutes, the struggling parts inside us know that someone cares, someone is paying attention. Beginning to notice, acknowledge, and accept our inner-feeling-worlds requires practicing away from the normal nonstop busyness of everyday life. By practicing the following four steps in a quiet place, you will become more able to practice them when the kids are bouncing off the walls, dinner is late, and you're exhausted from a busy day at work.

1. Be present to your inner self.
2. Accept that you have needs.
3. Attune to what is needed.
4. To the best of your ability, meet your needs.

Whenever your awareness settles on your inner self, allow it to expand to fully notice your experience in the moment—the sensations in your body, the thoughts in your head, and your emotional state. You don't need to try to change your experience. It's just helpful to become aware of what's going on.

We rarely want to be "fixed." We long to be understood and accepted.

Once the idea of giving yourself time out has settled just a bit into your consciousness, it will be easier in times of stress for that critical pause to happen, the pause that creates the space for you to fully experience yourself, as well as your loved ones.

Jan and Alix's Story, Continued

As I began to look inside and ask myself what I was feeling, I saw these emotions:

~ anger at my burdens: my job, single parenthood, my daughter's "bad" behavior

~ sadness and hurt that she would treat me this way
~ hate for the whole situation and resistance toward it
~ despair because this was not an acceptable way to be
  with my daughter

On top of that, physically I was feeling tired and hungry.

Once I could look at my own feelings, it was easy to see that Alix behaved as she did because her feelings were not too different from mine:

~ anger that she had to be "good" all day
~ sadness because she missed me and needed my attention
~ safety in my presence to express herself after enduring the restraints of school all day

As for physical feelings, she was tired and hungry, too.

Paying attention, and accepting both my own feelings and my daughter's dissolved my tightness and resistance, and allowed me to open to other possibilities. I finally acknowledged my feelings and fully accepted them as being okay. I fully acknowledged my daughter's feelings by asking her how she was doing and by letting her know it was okay to feel the way she did.

We also treated our trip home differently—I prepacked a nutritious snack and we went to a park near Alix's school before starting the drive home. This became a wonderful new routine! I was able to drop my previous belief that this was impossible because I didn't have time, because I had to get home and cook, do laundry, make calls, etc.

Because we had both let go of so much suffering, we were energized by the new experience and arrived home happy and relaxed. How I am with myself has made the difference. For me, the world has become a much friendlier place.

Sitting in Happy

Denise Roy

Denise Roy is a graduate of a Jesuit seminary, a mother of four, and the author of a book on motherhood called My Monastery Is a Minivan. *Here she writes about experiencing the sacred in the midst of ordinary family life.*

~

IF YOU WERE TO VISIT MY HOUSE, it's likely I would offer you a seat in Happy. And you'd probably agree with me—it *is* a wonderful place to sit.

Happy is the name of the half-leather, half-vinyl, dark blue rocker-recliner in our family room. It was my favorite place to nurse my daughter, Julianna, when she was a baby. Those moments were wonderful. I had no choice but to slow down, breathe, and relax enough so that the letdown reflex would work. She would nurse for a few seconds, peeking at me out of the corner of her eye, excited that she finally had my full attention. But she'd smile so much that she'd release the suction. Various games would then begin, including "Make a Face," "Smell My Feet," and "Bonk

Mom's Head." There are few experiences in life that equal that little mutual love-in.

When Julianna was just a little more than a year old, she somehow intuited the meaning of the word *happy*, knowing that it had a lot to do with whatever was happening in that chair. So one day, instead of making the little clicking sound she usually made whenever she wanted to nurse, she looked up at me, pointed to the chair, and said, "Happy." That was the christening of the chair, and we have called it by that name ever since.

I no longer have a little one tugging at my leg, begging me to "sit in Happy." When I did, it was easier for me to remember to stop and sit, to come back to the present moment and simply breathe. But there are times when I still hear a little voice, this one from inside myself, pulling at my heart and asking me to sit in Happy.

When I listen to the voice and make the choice to pause in my rapid journey through space and time, I find home again. In that place, I remember who I am. I connect with my body by slowing down my breathing. In that moment, there is nothing else to do, nowhere else to go. Very often, I practice the simple breathing meditation described by Buddhist monk Thich Nhat Hanh:

Breathing in, I calm my body.
Breathing out, I smile.
Dwelling in the present moment,
I know this is a wonderful moment!

No matter what is happening, I can smile. I can know that this is a wonderful moment. There is no desiring of anything; it is a place of quiet joy.

Thousands of years ago, the psalmist put into words the feeling of sitting in Happy:

> Lord, my heart is not proud;
>> nor are my eyes haughty.
> I do not busy myself with great matters,
>> with things too sublime for me.
> Rather, I have stilled my soul,
>> hushed it like a weaned child.
> Like a weaned child on its mother's lap,
>> so is my soul within me.

Psalm 131

When I sit in Happy and become centered, my children are drawn into this place as well. One day, Julianna and I were sitting quietly together in the chair. Then David, my eighteen-year-old son, ran over and draped his six-foot-one-inch body across us both. He was leaving for college the next week; as he sat on my lap, he gave me a hug, pretending he was still my little boy. We knew that life would soon be very different, and we all smiled in our awareness of that moment as a wonderful moment. Then his girlfriend knocked at the door, and he jumped up; the moment moved on, yet it stays in my heart.

Any chair, at any moment, can be Happy. Whenever we choose to sit in Happy, we come back to center again. We align ourselves with the love that patiently waits for us to slow down, pause, and invite it in. When we still and quiet our souls within us, we discover that we've never been separate from God or from one another. We experience the connection to all that is.

CONTRIBUTORS

ANDREA J. BUCHANAN is the author of *Mother Shock: Loving Every (Other) Minute of It* and a writer whose work has appeared in *Breeder: Real-Life Stories from the New Generation of Mothers* and in various online parenting magazines.

DAPHNE DE MARNEFFE, PhD, is a clinical psychologist, mother of three, and the author of *Maternal Desire: On Children, Love, and the Inner Life.* She lives with her family in California.

In her life B.C. (before children), CHERYL DIMOF worked as an occupational therapist. She currently lives in Kingston, Washington, with her husband, Ted, and her two children. She helps at preschool, chauffeurs her kids around, occasionally writes articles, and runs an Internet directory featuring family-friendly links and articles.

SUSAN J. DOUGLAS is the Catherine Neafie Kellogg Professor of Communications Studies at the University of Michigan. She is the coauthor, with Meredith W. Michaels, of *The Mommy Myth: The Idealization of Motherhood and How It Has Undermined Women.* She lives in Ann Arbor, Michigan, with her husband and daughter.

MEREDITH W. MICHAELS teaches philosophy at Smith College and writes about ethics and ideologies of reproduction and parenthood. She and her husband have five children and live in Amherst, Massachusetts.

LOUISE ERDRICH is a noted novelist and poet. She is the author of numerous books including *Four Souls, The Master Butchers Singing Club, Love Medicine,* and *The Blue Jay's Dance: A Birth Year.*

RABBI NANCY FUCHS-KREIMER, mother of two, is director of religious studies at the Reconstructionist Rabbinical College in Philadelphia, where she also teaches. She is the author of *Parenting as a Spiritual Journey: Deepening Ordinary and Extraordinary Events into Sacred Occasions.*

CAROLYN R. GIMIAN received a PhD in Early Childhood Education from the Union Graduate School—"in another life," as she puts it. For the last twenty-nine years, she has been an editor of the works of Tibetan meditation master Chögyam Trungpa. Carolyn lives in Halifax, Nova Scotia, with her husband, Jim. Her daughter is a freshman in college.

ARIEL GORE is the founder and editor of *Hip Mama,* an award-winning zine covering the culture and politics of motherhood. She is the author of several books including *The Mother Trip: Hip Mama's Guide to Staying Sane in the Chaos of Motherhood* and *Whatever, Mom: Hip Mama's Guide to Raising a Teenager.*

MIRIAM GREENSPAN is an internationally known psychotherapist, writer, and speaker who has helped to define the field of women's psychology. She is the author of *Healing Through the Dark Emotions: The Wisdom of Grief, Fear, and Despair* and *A New Approach to Women and Therapy*. She lives in Boston with her husband and two daughters.

NANCY HATHAWAY, MEd, is a therapist who has developed a popular training program for parents called Being Present with Our Children. She is also a senior dharma teacher in the Kwan Um School of Zen. She teaches meditation at the Cambridge Zen Center, in Cambridge, Massachusetts, and at the Morgan Bay Zendo in Surry, Maine. She is the mother of two boys, Christian and Jamie.

HARVILLE HENDRIX, PhD, in partnership with his wife, HELEN LAKELLY HUNT, PhD, originated Imago Relationship Therapy, a healing process for couples and parents. Hendrix is the author of the best-selling *Getting the Love You Want*. Hendrix and Hunt have a blended family with six children and are the coauthors of *Giving the Love That Heals: A Guide for Parents*.

CHERI HUBER has been a student and teacher of Zen for over thirty years. She teaches at the Zen Monastery Practice Center in Murphys, California, where she holds workshops and retreats. She is the author of seventeen books including *There Is Nothing Wrong with You* and *The Depression Book*, and she is the coauthor, with Melinda Guyol, of *Time-Out for Parents: A Guide to Compassionate Parenting*. MELINDA GUYOL is a licensed marriage and family therapist and a senior monk at the Zen Monastery Practice Center.

JON KABAT-ZINN is executive director of the Center for Mindfulness in Medicine, Health Care, and Society and associate professor of medicine at the University of Massachusetts Medical Center. He is the author of *Full Catastrophe Living* and *Wherever You Go, There You Are*. MYLA KABAT-ZINN has worked as a childbirth educator, birthing assistant, and environmental advocate. The Kabat-Zinns are the parents of three children.

KATRINA KENISON is a book editor and the author of *Mitten Strings for God: Reflections for Mothers in a Hurry*. She lives outside Boston with her husband and two sons.

HARRIET LERNER is an internationally acclaimed expert on women's psychology. She is the author of *The Dance of Anger, The Dance of Intimacy, The Dance of Connection, The Mother Dance,* and, most recently, *The Dance of Fear*. She is the mother of two sons and lives in Lawrence, Kansas.

CAROLYN MAGNER MASON is a freelance writer who lives with her family in Tuscaloosa, Alabama.

MUFFY MEAD-FERRO is the author of *Confessions of a Slacker Mom* and is an advertising copywriter and creative director. She lives with her husband and two children in Salt Lake City, Utah.

WENDY MOGEL, PhD, is a nationally known clinical psychologist, educator, and workshop leader. She is the mother of two girls and the author of *The Blessing of a Skinned Knee: Using Jewish Teachings to Raise Self-Reliant Children*.

JOAN K. PETERS has written for *The New York Times, Ms., Family Life, Cosmopolitan,* and *The Nation*. She is the author of *When Mothers Work: Loving Our Children Without Sacrificing Ourselves*.

ADRIENNE RICH is a distinguished poet and a recipient of the National Book Award. She is the author of more than seventeen volumes of poetry and five works of nonfiction including the landmark *Of Woman Born: Motherhood as Experience and Institution.*

ANNE ROIPHE is a noted novelist and journalist. She is the author of several books including *Fruitful: Living the Contradictions: A Memoir of Motherhood.*

DENISE ROY is a mother of four, a psychotherapist, and the founder of FamilySpirit, an organization that nurtures spirituality in families. She received a master of divinity degree from the Jesuit School of Theology in Berkeley, California, and is the author of *My Monastery Is a Minivan: Where Daily Is Divine and the Routine Becomes Prayer.* She lives in the San Francisco Bay Area.

SANDI KAHN SHELTON is the author of *Sleeping Through the Night and Other Lies* and *You Might As Well Laugh: Surviving the Joys of Parenthood,* a collection of humor columns, many of which appeared in *Working Mother* magazine. She's married and is the mother of three.

CREDITS

"One Week until College" by Sandi Kahn Shelton first appeared in Salon .com, at www.Salon.com, Sept. 8, 1997. An online version remains in the Salon archives. Reprinted with permission.

PART TWO: THE INNER WORK OF MOTHERHOOD

"Dawn" is excerpted from *Our Share of Night, Our Share of Morning* by Nancy Fuchs-Kreimer (available in paperback under the title *Parenting as a Spiritual Journey*). Copyright © 1996 by Nancy Fuchs-Kreimer. Reprinted by permission of HarperCollins Publishers Inc.

"Children as Spiritual Teachers" by Cheryl Dimof originally appeared in *Mothering Magazine* (May–June 2004). Reprinted by permission of the author and *Mothering Magazine*.

"Responding to 'Bad' Behavior" is reprinted with the permission of Scribner, an imprint of Simon & Schuster Adult Publishing Group, from *The Blessing of a Skinned Knee: Using Jewish Teachings to Raise Self-Reliant Children* by Wendy Mogel. Copyright © 2001 by Wendy Mogel, PhD.

"Parenting with Mindful Awareness" is reprinted from *Everyday Blessings* by Myla and Jon Kabat-Zinn. Copyright © 1997 by Myla Kabat-Zinn and Jon Kabat-Zinn. Reprinted by permission of Hyperion.

"Recognizing Our Hidden Wounds" is reprinted with the permission of Atria Books, an imprint of Simon & Schuster Adult Publishing Group, from *Giving the Love That Heals: A Guide for Parents* by Harville Hendrix, PhD and Helen Hunt. Copyright © 1997 by Harville Hendrix. All rights reserved.

" 'Exceptional' Mothering in a 'Normal' World" by Miriam Greenspan was adapted from her essay in *Mothering Against the Odds: Diverse Voices of Contemporary Mothers,* edited by Cynthia Garcia Coll et al. New York: The Guilford Press, 1998. Reprinted by permission of Guilford Press.

CREDITS

PART THREE: WHY IS BEING A MOTHER SO HARD?

"Guilt—What It Does to Us," excerpts from *Fruitful* by Anne Roiphe. Copyright © 1996 by Anne Roiphe. Reprinted by permission of International Creative Management, Inc. and the Houghton Mifflin Company.

"The New Momism" is reprinted with the permission of The Free Press, a Division of Simon & Schuster Adult Publishing Group, from *The Mommy Myth: The Idealization of Motherhood and How It Has Undermined Women* by Susan J. Douglas and Meredith W. Michaels. Copyright © 2004 by Susan Douglas and Meredith Michaels. All rights reserved.

"Power Moms and the Problem of Overparenting" is reprinted from *When Mothers Work* by Joan K. Peters. Copyright © 1997 by Joan K. Peters. Reprinted by permission of Da Capo, a member of Perseus Books, L.L.C., and by arrangement with Joan Peters c/o Writers House as agent for the proprietor, New York, NY.

"Claiming the Joy" is reprinted from *Maternal Desire* by Daphne de Marneffe. Copyright © 2004 by Daphne de Marneffe. By permission of Little, Brown and Company, Inc.

PART FOUR: FINDING BALANCE

"Tell Your Secrets" is reprinted from *The Mother Trip: Hip Mama's Guide to Staying Sane in the Chaos of Motherhood* by Ariel Gore. Copyright © 2000 by Ariel Gore. Reprinted by permission of Seal Press.

"Simplicity" is reprinted from *Mitten Strings for God* by Katrina Kenison. Copyright © 2000 by Katrina Kenison. By permission of Warner Books, Inc.

The first section of "I'm Breathing, Are You?" by Nancy Hathaway originally appeared in *Buddhadharma: The Practitioner's Quarterly*, Fall 2002.

"Good-bye Herd" is reprinted from *Confessions of a Slacker Mom* by Muffy Mead-Ferro. Copyright © 2004 by Muffy Mead-Ferro. Reprinted by permission of Da Capo, a member of Perseus Books, L.L.C.